To Melinda,

Find your voice!

Speak out!

Dr. Reni

SUFFERING
IN SILENCE

Break the Silence

Let the suffering End...Let Healing Begin

SUFFERING
IN SILENCE

Break the Silence

Let the suffering End...Let Healing Begin

Renee Fowler Hornbuckle

Suffering in Silence

Break the Silence: Let Suffering End...Let Healing Begin

Edition
Copyright © 2012 by Renee Fowler Hornbuckle

Library of Congress Catalog – in Publication Data

ISBN 978-1480171664

Printed in the United States of America

Published by Jabez Books
(A Division of Clark's Consultant Group)
www.clarksconsultantgroup.com

Unless otherwise noted, all Scripture quotations are taken from *The New King James Version, WORDsearch 7.0.* Copyright © 2007 WORDsearch Corp.

1. Domestic Violence – Religious -- Self-Esteem -- Christianity

Voices of Praise For

Suffering In Silence

"Suffering In Silence" is a very powerful must read for ALL those who feel trapped in the cycle of domestic violence. Pastor Renee Hornbuckle is to be applauded for this fascinating book that is not only revealing but a great teaching tool. This book teaches the reader how to recognize the symptoms of an abusive relationship and provides the tools to break-out. As a veteran law enforcement officer with over 25 years of experience I would recommend this book to not only those who are caught in the cycle of domestic violence, but also to those who are trained to protect the victims. Kudos to you, Pastor Renee, for having the courage to end your own silence on this subject. This book will truly allow the suffering to end for those who read it and allow the healing process to begin!!!

James Hawthorne
Assistant Police Chief
Arlington (Texas) Police Department

"Bibliotherapy is widely used in professional and pastoral counseling for emotional healing. Dr. Renee's book, *Suffering in Silence,* provides a rare inside look at the traumatic effect and recovery from domestic violence in the eyes of a "first lady". It's a must read for counselors and clients in all settings. "

Freda D. Doxey LPC
Licensed Professional Counselor
The Doxey Group, Inc.

For 17 years, I served as a criminal court judge in the State of Texas. Within my tenure, I presided over 2000 cases annually, ranging from rape, assault, to murder.   However, when the Hornbuckle's ordeal made the news, my heart was truly saddened. I knew the Hornbuckle's for many years and after leaving the bench I provided legal services to Dr. Renee Hornbuckle and her church from time to time. Truly, their situation was a tragedy! Not just for them, but for the body of Christ as a whole. However, God is good at taking a mess and making a message. This is how I would characterize Dr. Renee Hornbuckle's book, ***"Suffering in Silence"***. It is a message of hope and inspiration for all who have and are going through a similar ordeal. **Suffering in Silence** is a healing balm for the ages. It is a rectifier and reconciler for the disenfranchised. It is a clarion call for our nation's wounded. But most of all, it is a prophetic voice for those that are *still* suffering in silence that need a voice to deliver them. **Every man, woman, pastor, minister, husband and wife need to read this book!** I highly recommend this literary work. This masterpiece has been pinned from the canvas of a broken and marred heart, but yet refined. Kudos, Dr. Renee for your resilience and your ability to forgive for you are truly that 'Woman of Influence' you often laud over others. May God continue to bless you and keep you!

Attorney Faith Johnson
Law Office of Faith Johnson and Associates
Former Texas Criminal District Judge

While serving as a judge of a family violence court for seven years, I had the opportunity to see how domestic violence transcended every race, culture and social economic background. In **"Suffering in Silence,"** Pastor Renee Hornbuckle not only shares her personal experience as a victim of violence, she encourages others to recognize the patterns of abuse and gives them the strength to face their own circumstances. I encourage you to read this book. It might change your life or give you the tools to help someone else change theirs.

Attorney Dianne Jones McVay
Law Office of Dianne Jones McVay
Former Dallas County Judge, State of Texas

As if we are a valued guest in her home, Renee Hornbuckle walks the reader through her life. The conversation is informal and casual, relaxed and open, but there is an urgency conveyed. As the story unfolds, you realize that the story is a cautionary tale told with courage and the intention to protect the reader from the horrors she came to know intimately. As she leads you through her private suffering like rooms being unlocked, she shows you the secrets that will lock you in if her tips go unheeded. Giving practical guidance, clues, and hidden hints she warns the reader of the telltale signs of unhealthy relationships breaking her silence to rescue others.

It is common for victims of domestic violence to be silent, and very few find their voice to recount the psychological warfare waged against them;

10

but when an admired, highly respected leader discloses her story and breaks her silence, the hope is that others, too, will find their voice and break their silence.

This story of triumph over unimaginable betrayal will help countless women, men and children who have suffered in silence. This book is for you If you want information to help you in identifying, recognizing and taking action to protect yourself and others from the evils of domestic violence.

This is a real life comeback story for anyone wanting to gain insight into a touching account of tragedy and triumph. Renee Hornbuckle has broken her silence, walked through healing and gotten her voice back. Her voice is the voice of a champion! As a mental healthcare provider, I highly recommend this book as a resource tool for other providers and victims of domestic violence.

Yvette J. Munroe
Chief Executive Officer
Covenant Community Partners, LLC

Dr Renee hits the enemy straight on by releasing this well written bomb shell! Now women around the nations and the globe can be free to break their silence and suffer no more! Freedom has come in the form of a woman who said she will no longer allow suffering to keep her from fulfilling her God given gifts, talents and purposes in the earth! Now the nations will see countless women breathing, healing and releasing their silence! Wonderful and Sensational!

Apostle Christopher J Hardy
International Covenant Life Network
International Covenant Connect
Eagles International Business Institute

Suffering in Silence is a book that is Real, Relevant, and Relatable. Renee Hornbuckle has pinned her journey from a life of suffering to a life of freedom. Her transparency in the pages of this book gives you a genuine feel of each experience. This book is filled with hands on tools that can help you look inside of yourself and discover the hidden "YOU", and help you walk in freedom and not fear. What has been concealed can now be healed. I highly recommend that this book gets in the hands of anyone who is ready to break the silence and live the life that he or she was designed to live.

Tyrone Lister
International Speaker & Best Selling Author
www.TyroneLister.com

Thank You!

You are all loved and appreciated!

My Family for their unwavering support.

My true friends who stood beside me and encouraged me every step of the way.

My Congregation and Community who by standing with me forced me to not give up and stand up for what was right.

The host of Ministers, Counselors and Life Coaches who helped me heal, advised me and gave insight to this project.

And to the Women and Men who have allowed me to minister to them and who shared their stories. This is what truly gave me the courage to step up and share mine!

Love you all more!

Table of Contents

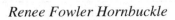

SILENCE

There are times in our lives when SILENCE is useful. There are other times when it is not. The role and value of SILENCE depends on our experiences as well as the intended outcome and purpose.

SILENCE is defined as:

<u>Noun</u>

1. The state or quality of being silent.

2. The absence of sound or noise; stillness.

3. Refusal or failure to speak, communicate, etc., when expected.

4. A period of time without noise.

5. Oblivion or obscurity.

<u>Verb</u>

1. To bring to silence.

2. To put a stop to; extinguish: to silence all complaints.

As you can see, by definition, *silence* has positive and negative attributes. On the positive side, "the absence of sound or noise" can restore us, giving us the opportunity to slow down, find rest, and be at peace. These times of productive silence help us to clear our thoughts, quiet our inner person, and find our creative voice. Also, in this productive silence, there is no fear, only a sense of quiet joy and calmness as perspective is regained and aligned in our spirit, soul and body. These are wonderful times—productive silence-- healing silence.

On the other hand, when we look at silence from its negative tenet, it can be divisive and destructive. Interwoven in this component of silence, are things that are harbored that often need to be exposed, such as fear, shame, humiliation, abuse and embarrassment to name a few. And it is in this type of silence that communication is in dire need.

You see, this kind of silence is counterproductive and can even be dangerous. However, one of the primary reasons many people choose to keep this type of silence concealed is because this "silence" convinces many that they must remain silent to protect the people they love. As well, they often feel responsible for the situation; therefore, exposing these random acts of maladies is not an option.

THIS TYPE OF SILENCE WILL ALWAYS CAUSE SUFFERING!

This type of counterproductive silence must be exposed! If not exposed and if it continues to be treated like a "secret," it will eventually cause unnecessary pain in everyone's life who is involved and/or connected.

I know this first hand, which I have chronicled in this book. For many years of my marriage, off and on, I had to endure counterproductive silence. The lessons I have learned through my ordeal, are that one can only be truly healed when the **SILENCE IS BROKEN.**

We live in a chaotic world that seems to be going crazy! Countless people from all walks of life—women, boys, and girls, men included also—are suffering unnecessarily. Almost daily we hear unbelievable stories of people being abused, and others doing all types of heinous (monstrous, shocking) acts that induce suffering. The media is flooded with news about everyday people as well as celebrities, politicians, entertainers, athletes, clergymen and others who are suffering. But the sad fact about this is those who cause suffering typically do so because they have suffered in the past or are still suffering.

This isn't an excuse, but it's all too common that "hurt people *hurt* people." It is also a popular saying that "misery loves company." When someone is suffering, the act of causing others to suffer is likely to occur. This destructive cycle, and the silent cries it creates, needs to be broken.

As you read my story, I want you to consider your own life. And as you think about your life, and you find your life mirroring some of the things I am sharing in this book, I want you to stop, breath, slow down, and shut out all the noises in your life. Regain your composure, then begin to reflect on my experiences, and hopefully, this will help you initiate a moment of respite.

In this resting state, I want you to have a pad or journal and pen on hand. When you come to the **"Breaking Free – Break the Silence"** tips and exercises at the end of each chapter, take a deep breath, pray and let the truth from your heart flow onto the paper. Refuse to conceal anything that is painful and counterproductive.

My prayer is that by reading this book you will find the strength to break your silence **and** suffering. I hope you will find the courage to speak out and change your situation. And finally, it is my prayer also that you will be able to regain the life you once loved, so you can truly live again.

No one, and I do mean no one, should have to ***suffer in silence***. Now, let's get prepared and situated, so you will be ready to get started.

Let your healing begin by breaking the SILENCE!

Let's begin the journey.

We gain strength, and courage, and confidence by each experience in which we really stop to look fear in the face... we must do that which we think we cannot.

Eleanor Roosevelt

27

Chapter 1

SHATTERED SILENCE

The Day That Changed My Life Forever

The walls in the room seemed as though they were caving in on me. My hands were clammy and my mind was thinking all types of things. Maybe I had been in the hotel room for an hour or 15 minutes, I didn't know any more. All I knew, I was told earlier by my husband to go into one room in the hotel, while he met with a team of legal experts and leaders in another room.

As I was in the room, I was trying to think of all the variables that possibly my husband and the legal team and leaders were discussing. However, I was previously aware of a pending legal action that was going on, but even with this, I was not fully aware of the intricate details. But just thinking about this on this day also became a frustration for me. All sorts of thoughts kept flowing in and out and through my mind. Constantly, my mind was bombarded with thoughts of skepticisms and suppositions.

One time I thought; perhaps, someone was trying to sue the church or was trying to harass us in some form for their personal financial gain. You see, my husband and I had been pastoring over

15 years, and we always believed and taught that God wanted His people to prosper. We took many "hits" for this, but God honored our faithfulness. And because of this, He blessed us abundantly, so that we eventually became financially independent.

Also, our church sat on approximately 14 acres of land, with a compound of almost 50,000 square feet, which included a 28,000 square foot main building. Within this building housed a sanctuary (seating capacity/1000 people); full service gym (10,000 Square feet); arcade room for the youth; a full service nursery (with the capacity for 200 kids); numerous executive suites and an educational extension. In addition, we also owned 16 acres of land adjacent to this facility.

During this span in our lives, we also owned two businesses; were authors of several publications, were motivational speakers (that traveled extensively), and we managed several other financial generating entities and non-profit organizations.

However, I quickly dismissed this thought, but then I thought if not this perhaps it is something else. My emotions and thoughts were "all over the place."

At another point, I found myself surfing the internet looking up all types of rehab centers, thinking perhaps, that it might even be a possibility my husband needed an intervention of sorts to address the peculiar behaviors that he had exhibited within the past few years; that had apparently landed us here in this moment. Bottom line, I didn't know what to think. So over and over again, I repeated this cycle, trying to think of scenarios of the real reason why I was held at bay in this room instead of being in the room with my husband and the others.   But nothing I conjured up in that room could have ever prepared me for what I was getting ready to encounter and endure.

What In The World Was Really Wrong?

THAT DAY!

This was not the norm!

You see, it was a beautiful Sunday morning, my birthday, January 9, 2005 to be exact. Our family was headed to church like any other Sunday. By all external indications, we were the picture perfect family: A strong man, a smart woman, and three wonderful children. We had everything that attributed to success: a beautiful home, luxury cars, money and influence.

This Sunday neither my husband nor I were scheduled to preach, we had a guest speaker. Also, our Bishop (a leader who provided oversight to our ministry) was in town. As we approached the door of our offices, it was apparent something was wrong.

What happened afterwards is somewhat a blur still in my mind. When we arrived together, I was asked to go with my husband to a local hotel where legal counsel and other accountability partners were waiting for us. So I made provision for our children and our guests and headed to the hotel. When we arrived, my husband went into a hotel room and he asked me to wait in another room while he met with everyone else. So I stayed in the hotel room until it was over.

When he returned, every question I asked irritated him greatly. With an intense anger and aggression that deeply concerned me. He said some people were still falsely accusing him of some horrendous acts. Again, I was aware of an allegation, but was not privy to the severity of the situation. But one thing became clear to me on that day; this was not the time to question or cross-examine my husband. So I watched and kept my distance.

THAT DAY my life changed forever.

THAT DAY I realized there had been a downward spiral in our lives for years.

THAT DAY I questioned the person I had married. Who was he? Why was all this happening? What was really going on?

Full Disclosure, Opening Pandora's Box

It wasn't long after this that everything unfolded. My husband, who I had been married to for 17 years and with whom I had co-founded our church nineteen years before was being accused of sexually assaulting three of our female church members, and drugging two of them. Added to that, he was facing a separate drug charge from when the police reportedly found drugs and a glass pipe in his car during his arrest. Needless to say, it was an overwhelmingly difficult time for me.

During the months that followed, however, I stood beside my husband trying to believe in what he said. I supported him in the midst of these horrific attacks, even though everything else around us was falling apart. We even had press conferences, which I reluctantly participated in as well. Reluctant because I had no idea of what the truth was.

This ordeal was no small matter. The situation became a headliner on national news. I can recall seeing a tag line on one of the national news stations about my husband's pending allegations as I sat on the edge of my bed. I was shocked! I was mortified! This was no laughing matter. This entire situation was life-shattering! The next few years (2005 and 2006) were a nightmare for me and my family! Forever etched in my mind.

It has been seven years since this calamity occurred. And because of one man's actions, many people had to endure much anguish and stress. While this was a tremendous strain and undertaking in my life and the life of my family, this book is not about who did what or how the circumstances unfolded, but it is more about my personal journey, the lessons I learned, and how God brought me through. It is also about my silence, the negative and positive silence, and how I regained my voice. Of course, to share my inward journey with you, I'll need to touch on certain aspects of what was happening in my world; many of them painful. But as you read this book, I want you to remember: **When you're facing challenges on every side, your response will determine your outcome.**

It is my hope that no matter what has taken place in your life that you'll start right now, right where you are, and put yourself in a posture to trust God and move forward—even if everything around you has been shattered. Remember, your journey of recovery will be a day-by-day, step-by-step process.

Once you get over the shock of a devastating blow you can begin to come to terms with your situation and your emotions. For me, this included taking a hard look within *myself* and at the things that had brought *me* to this point.

Are you ready to take this journey with me?

Here goes...

BREAKING FREE-BREAKING THE SILENCE TIP

Exercise: Feeling Safe

Feeling safe is the first step to breaking the silence. Since you did not feel safe during the trauma, you now have to intentionally create "safe items" or a "safe place". For this exercise, you need to identify, list and when possible gather any item that makes you feel safe. This could include any textured item (stuff animal, natural fiber item, etc.), a song, a jewelry item, a picture, crystal goblet, futon, or a place. Go ahead and write down your safe items or places. Re-read your list as God may give you other safe items or places to add to your list. When appropriate, keep your safe items nearby or go to your safe place.

My safe item(s): *ex: My safe place is my home with my peaceful music and my water fountains. It provides me a place of refuge.*

_____

_____

_____

_____

_____

_____

_____

_____

_____

_____

_____

_____

_____

BREAKING FREE-BREAKING THE SILENCE TIP

Exercise: Create Your "That Day" Event Chart

"That Day" events are those things or situations that remind you of the time your trauma occurred. In your "Breaking the Silence" journal, as the Holy Spirit guides you, list each of your "THAT DAY" event(s) in a chart (see chart provided).

It may be a challenge to recall any or all events. Also, recognize when the reminder of the trauma is too painful for you. When this happens, immediately, put down the pen and journal, go to your safe place or item(s) and pray to God asking Him to remind you of His Grand Protection over you.

Your "THAT DAY" chart should look something like this:

Event	My Thoughts	My Feelings	My Actions
He told me to quit my career if I loved him.	"He's right. I do love him."	Sad, lonely, unsure	I quit my career.

Life moves on, whether we act as
cowards or heroes.
Life has no other
discipline to impose,
if we would but realize it,
than to accept life unquestioningly.
Everything we shut our eyes to,
everything we run away from,
everything we deny,
denigrate or despise,
serves to defeat us in the end.
What seems nasty, painful, evil,
can become a source of beauty,
joy and strength,
if faced with an open mind.
Every moment is a golden one
for him who has the vision
to recognize it as such.

Henry Miller

Chapter 2

MY STORY

Control and Manipulation

G oing through an ordeal like my family went through in 2005, has a way of causing you to be reflective and to revisit and continually reevaluate your life's journey. When I began to look back over my life, I saw things I had never seen before or that I had

45

blocked out. Things that were once obscured became clear, but things that were somewhat visible became even more profound.

I had a great upbringing in a solid family with good morals and distinct values, where we were encouraged to always be contributing citizens to society. My family believed not just in setting goals, but in achieving goals. For me, this was a great foundation in my life to build upon to be successful in whatever I put my heart and mind to achieve. Life was good and it seemed as though everything was on track for my life.

I grew up in Little Rock, Arkansas, the youngest of five, all girls. My parents had me later in life – at age 40. The sister closest to me was eight years older, then a set of twins – eleven years older, and my oldest sister who was sixteen years older. I was considered the second generation of the family being that I was so much younger. The truth was that I was the last attempt for a boy in the family. But on January 9, 1962, another bubbly baby girl entered the world! Renee Denise Fowler, my given name. The family exuberantly (I'm told) welcomed me – their new bundle of joy!

Since I was the youngest, they all treated me as one would expect the youngest to be treated - as the baby. However, since I was so much younger, I was raised almost as an only child, so I was very mature and responsible, having been raised by older parents, yet, still very much the baby of the family.

I had a great relationship with both my parents and my sisters, as we were taught "family comes first after God". Even at a young age, they all recognized my natural maturity, wisdom and insight.   So, we would have wonderful life discussions. We were very much considered a normal, successful, middle class family as defined by the standards of that time. As well, we had the normal pressures that most families faced, and had to overcome. This taught me many life lessons. My parents were wonderful role models and so were my sisters. Me and my sisters, affectionately known as "The Fowler Girls" were also quite normal. Even with our love for each other and our age gaps, we experienced the normal ups and downs of how "siblings" relate. So, there were often "loving" disagreements that ensued, arguments over who took my shoes, who borrowed my clothes and threats of who was going to "tell."

Often my sisters would tease me about looking Chinese, and whether or not they would keep me, even though I was not the baby boy they had expected mama and daddy to bring home from the hospital. But overall, they loved me, along with my parents. They all helped to develop the strength I have and contributed to the woman that I am today.

My parents were trailblazing educators, who taught us to strive for excellence in all that we pursued. My father, the first African American, Assistant Superintendent of the Little Rock School District, and my mother was one of the first African American teachers to integrate schools. So the bar was always set high for us to achieve academically and in extra-curricular activities.

I was active in various student leadership and business programs, was a girl scout, played softball for nine years, took piano lessons, played the flute, and yes, I was a cheerleader and the mascot in high school. There was a lot of life and love in our household. So when I graduated from high school, I set off to conquer the world.

My Early Adult Years

It was first during my early young adult years when I recognized that my life took an unexpected turn.

I was a bright and shining young college student on the campus of the University of Arkansas with a great future ahead of me. Mesmerized by the campus (as most new students are), I was equally as influenced by the attention and affirmation of others. What I didn't know is that my experience there, and my perspective, was about to change. I was about to be introduced to the world of *SILENCE*.

You see, I met this wonderful, good looking top athlete on campus, and I was so excited. I should have known something was up when his ex-girlfriend approached me, letting me know to be careful in my dealings with him. Yet, as most of us would probably do, I shrugged her off as being a "hater." I paid no attention to her warning, reasoning to myself that she was just jealous. I convinced myself that she simply did not want me to have a good relationship with her ex-boyfriend. I felt I could be successful and handle this relationship where she had failed.

Five years later...

I was still in this relationship, and was well acquainted with the world of control and manipulation by now. A world that I had kept secret and now, it was about to explode. I should

51

have paid attention to all the signs, but I did not. I was in love. I also did not want people to know what I had endured. I was ashamed and in a state of emotional upheaval.

For most of those years, a question had been racing through my mind: *Have I been suffering?* After all, he had not actually abused me physically. But there had been so many mind games, emotional swings, and yes, verbal abuse. He did everything he could to control and manipulate me. This up-and-down roller coaster relationship definitely took away the joy in my life. My parents had cautioned me to stay away from men like this, and now I knew all too well that I definitely wasn't comfortable with this kind of life. It felt like I was suffering and alone, silently enduring the pain while masking a happy face for others.

On the day when I decided to call off our relationship, I was in for a shocking surprise (with controlling and manipulating people things have to go their way or no way). I will never forget that moment, while sharing my feelings; he became quite angry. He thrust his fist through a wall in an uncontrollable rage. FEAR gripped my heart. I felt "fear" like I had never felt fear before. Every beat in my heart, I could hear and feel.

Of course, he apologized for doing it. He told me that he would never do that again, or ever do anything to me for that matter. But something inside me said, "Next time it will be you." I stood my ground and called off the relationship.

For awhile he stayed away. Then periodically I started seeing him show up wherever I was, glaring at me from across the room, the restaurant or the mall. I could not believe it. Now someone was stalking me! Oh my God, how could this be?

Finally, while I was at a friend's house one day, the door flew off the hinges. My ex-boyfriend had kicked the door in to get to me! Then my friend pulled out a gun. I thought, *"This is it! No one should have to live this way."* I had been in this abusive relationship for five long years and he still wanted to control my life. But it was time for me to move on.

Too ashamed to tell my family or friends what I had been going through, I moved silently and quickly, quitting my job and moving to Texas. Think about that...Never telling a soul! I made a major geographical move to start a new life to get away from a crazy person! And I made sure to move far away, where I felt this dangerous

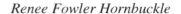

relationship could not follow or threaten me ever again.

I liked Texas and landed a great job in Corporate Training and Development. Then after one month, my father and my grandmother died one week apart. The grief was overwhelming. I took time off from my new job, headed home to Arkansas to bury my father, and then went to North Carolina to bury my grandmother. I had to dig deep for inner strength to help my family get through this difficult time. I realized, once again, I was faced with making a major decision.

My first instinct was to remain in Arkansas to be near my mother, but we decided it would be best for me to return to Texas and pursue my dreams. So that is what I did. For the next two years I kept focused on advancing my career.

A Brand-New, Exciting Life

Things finally fell into place and life could not have been better. I was a young, successful corporate woman climbing the ladder to success! Still, I felt empty inside, like there was a void. This void caused me to do some deep soul-searching and personal reflection. I'm so thankful for that empty feeling, because after years of searching, I finally found what I was looking for—an authentic relationship with Jesus Christ.

I had reached a place in my life where I realized that there was more to life than just a wild life of partying and making money. It was at this point of awareness that I realized I wanted more out of life, and I knew I had more to give. But in order to get to more, I knew there needed to be a total makeover of who I had become, so like many, I turned to God.

I had grown up in church with an awareness of God, however, I never really had a *right* (authentic) relationship with the Lord. I was fully aware through my upbringing that a personal relationship with Jesus was what I needed to get my life on the right path.

In my pursuit of getting my life right, I finally made the decision to seek out a church. I called my mother to ask her for the name of the church she had wanted me to attend when I first moved to Texas. She not only gave me the name of the church, but the pastor's name also. So, I joined the United Methodist church on the referral of my mother. Why the United Methodist Church? Because this was the spiritual environment I had been raised in and where I was most comfortable. And it had been a stable and consistent part of my upbringing.

So as I finally surrendered my life totally to the Lordship of Jesus, I eagerly began developing my spiritual life as much as I could so that I would be built up and confident to live a moral life. This was it! An authentic personal relationship with Jesus Christ! I enthusiastically committed to become a true disciple or learner of the Bible. I proudly made the commitment to follow Christ with great boldness in order to share the gospel with other people. I felt like I was on top of the world!

During these years, my co-workers were the closest people to me. They were the first to notice the transition in my life. I no longer attended happy hour with them, but I invited them to attend what I considered to be an even happier hour – Bible Study. I actively attended church and Bible study, and was no longer living a life built on riotous activities. My personal response to this higher call caused me to set a goal of becoming a faithful servant in my daily life. I sought to understand biblical truth and to grow in the Christian faith. A process that I knew would take discipline and study of the Bible. Finally, I had a good clean life, a great job, and was hanging out with great people!

A Match Made In Heaven

In the pursuit of my positive life transition, I met another man. He was leading the Bible study I was attending. He was single, and so was I and neither of us was dating anyone. His understanding and ability to teach the Word of God was astounding. Being that I had only one serious relationship before, which had not turned out so great, I was easily impressed by this man who appeared to be everything I desired. He had potential: vision, dream, ambition and big plans for the future—and he treated me like a queen. It was like a match made *in heaven.*

Our courtship was brief. After all, we were both active Christians and did not want to fall into sin. But once again, rumors and signs began to emerge. I heard that he had been married before for a brief time. I told myself lots of people have been married before, especially in this day and age, so I convinced myself that it was probably no big deal. But when I did ask about his marriage, no one would discuss it. Lips were sealed tight about the subject. In hindsight, I should have recognized this silence. It was like his marriage had never existed. So instead of pulling back, I overlooked the odd responses and thought, *"Well, I won't worry about it. It does not have anything to do with us."*

A few short months later, we were married. I was totally committed to the relationship, and no one could have told me that he wasn't who he proclaimed to be. After all, this one I met at church, and he was teaching and leading Bible study. Like he had done so passionately while we were dating, my husband continued to treat me like a queen and he worked hard to give me everything my heart desired. Unbeknownst to me, however, this wonderful life of love and romance was about to change.

My personal decision and response to ignore the warning signs determined the outcome I faced soon after. The truth is when you are swept into a whimsical world of romance with "the perfect" man, it is hard to be objective. That is why it is important to listen to others—in my case, even family members and ex-girlfriends. We have to develop the ability to *hear* and *heed* warnings, whether they are spoken out loud or are revealed through uncomfortable SILENCE.

Proverbs 11:14 says, *"Where there is no counsel, the people fall; but in the multitude of counselors there is safety."*

Now hear me. As long as there is life in you, there is hope. Like me, you may have made unwise decisions that led to heartbreak and even disaster. But you can break free from that cycle. God doesn't want you to suffer. He wants you to be safe in the counsel of His Word, and surrounded by caring, godly people who will tell you the truth in love.

So heed my advice, press on and believe God for change in your life even if you are in a bad situation right now.

You will have to open your eyes and assess your situation looking objectively at where it all began, so you can start to identify what is needed to change your situation. With the help of wise people and support you can learn to break your SILENCE and regain your life.

BREAKING FREE – BREAKING THE SILENCE TIP

EXERCISE: Who Will You Be Accountable To?

It is nearly impossible to know everything about ourselves, let alone another person. When you are in a romantic relationship, your thoughts, feelings and even your body fully participate in the romance. Times of romance are times for us to be committed to an accountability group of believers. Responsibility and accountability go hand in hand. I operate responsibly and I am accountable to "the counsel of many" (Proverbs 11:14).

In this exercise, I suggest you make a list of three to five individuals you will be accountable to in every area of your life. This list would include but not limited to a godly person who is, a same sex peer, a professional in your area of work, an elder, a seasoned couple (if you are married), your pastoral leader, etc. With each person, ask them if they will be your accountability partner in a specific area of your life.

Three questions you should be willing to answer and be transparent about are:

1. Tell of any consistent unrighteous thoughts, beliefs or plans/actions toward self or others?
2. Reveal any ungodly deeds done for self and/or others?
3. How are you doing in the two areas since your last meeting?

I suggest you meet once a month, face-to-face at an agreed upon area.

Use your journal to record your actions so that you can see your progress and celebrate your growth.

Your life and spiritual growth will abound tremendously. So, enjoy the process of honestly assessing your life!

Chapter 3

ENTERING

INTO SILENCE

The Early Years of Marriage

We were always greeted with kindness, affection and love as we attended our pre-marital counseling sessions. We would meet at my apartment and ride to the sessions together. Often the sessions were scheduled for evenings after work. We were always on time and eager to hear what the pastor was going to share with us. We were in love and we wanted the best for our marriage, *so I thought.*

"Hello, Terry and Renee, how are you doing today? How was your week? Is everything okay?" The pastor would ask. Every session was greeted with such pleasantries as these. He would go over certain information with us and ask us questions, then at the appointed time we would join the others in group sessions. I can't express to you how eager and thrilled I was to know that I was going to be somebody's wife – *Terry Hornbuckle's wife.* My heart was constantly in a fluttered state.

But it did not take long for me to realize that most of our counseling sessions were about "fixing" me. Yet, I was eager to learn all I could about marriage and what was required by God's guidelines. As a strong, independent, professional woman, it was important for me to fully understand God's expectation of me as a wife. I so wanted to get it right! Therefore, I put in the time that was needed to get things together so that I could emerge as the model wife!

Thinking back on these days now is like a vapor in my mind. The hours we spent meeting with the pastoral team and the things we talked about specifically elude my thoughts. But, for some odd reason, again what I am vividly able to recall is that the majority of the time was spent "fixing" me.

I think it is fair to say that within our 22 years of marriage and ministry, there were good times and bad times; up and down times. I learned a lot of positive things that contribute to **who I am today**, but there also were many negative things that contributed to **where I am today**.

When we first met; of course, my now ex-husband was my prince charming. He was different. A man with potential, and as I stated earlier, he had a vision, a dream, and he treated me like a queen. We had a whirlwind courtship, but we wanted to do things God's way, that's why we married a few months after we met.

The day of our wedding was in the fall, November, a beautiful season in Arkansas. My sisters teased me and said I was having a *"show"*. I had eleven bridesmaids and junior bridesmaids. Being the youngest of the five girls, and with my father being deceased, everyone pitched in to help coordinate and to finance our wedding. It was nothing short of "grande" – a true fairy tale wedding. A "grande" beginning to what I expected to be nothing less, than a "grande" future!

Together we seemed unstoppable! I was hooked in and committed to the end. You could not have told me that he wasn't either. He treated me like a queen by working hard to please me. However, during those pre-marital sessions and shortly after the wedding, the honeymoon fantasy began to decrease, and overwhelming expectations began to replace the romance. For instance, constant demands, the dictatorial orders I was expected to follow or else I was not being a "good" wife. This was slowly integrated into my thinking and daily life, so I grew accustomed to living in this manner. The baffling thing is, during those years, I did not recognize what was really happening; that I was being made or molded into being a subservient wife.

Our lives took off at a fast pace, things began to really fall into place, and rapidly we rose to the top as a successful couple. I believe some of what contributed to what I did not see had to do with my zeal in trying to be a godly wife and a pastor's wife. Then later, the responsibility of children, ministry and other duties that came with being a public figure consumed me.

So I got busy, I didn't slow down, and I *overlooked* many things. I didn't fully comprehend how drastically things had really changed in my life until just a few years ago. I guess I finally awakened! It has taken until now for me to look back and see all the negative and unhealthy patterns that were happening within the relationship. You would think that once someone has seen and experienced manipulation and control that they would not buy into it again.

But the face of manipulation and control will package itself differently each time. It is often difficult to discern. And this time it was packaged as charismatic, suave and with the promise of a fairy tale life (which I have lived, and it was great – but at a price).

I believed so strongly in everything (marriage, what my role was supposed to be as a wife, what my husband should do, etc) from the beginning; not knowing or seeing that each day a part of me was taken away.

Over the years, my husband's manipulation progressed. It started out as what I termed "simple" manipulation (doing things to get his way), and then became more domineering and

73

controlling; finally, isolation and abandonment ensued - verbal, emotional and mental suffering was eventually the norm.

For the ones that have gone through what I have experienced, according to statistics, this progression of behaviors is normal. We become enamored by the relationship and the other person so deeply that we overlook these negative proclivities. We get too close and are unable to see things for what they really are. That is where I found myself. I was too close to see the patterns of behavior that were being used against me to gain and maintain absolute power and control over me. Typically, a person who uses control and manipulation over their partner will display a pattern of behavior that is used to dominate the partner through all types of negative behaviors, which we will address in the next chapter.

Now, I realize that there was a lot of power and control in the form of intimidation, manipulation, and isolation that I allowed myself to be subjected to within the relationship. Nonetheless, that is how the cycle begins.

We enter the relationship with the idea of it being wonderful and healthy, and then we become a casualty of the unhealthy actions that occur. Next, we become ashamed, embarrassed, fearful, afraid or disappointed in ourselves that we ever allowed ourselves to be subjected to such behavior.

So rather than talk about it or expose it, we allow the cycle of inappropriate behaviors to continue. We hide behind a mask and **suffer in silence**. It is only when you make a choice and start taking the steps to break the silence, will you break the suffering and start the healing process!

75

When you are in it, you always make excuses and compensation for the other person's behavior whether you are female or male, young or old. It wasn't until later that the emotional, mental and verbal abuse finally turned to the physical abuse.

As the years progressed, I began to have concerns about my husband's behaviors, attitudes and schedules. I had not grown up with domestic abuse of any kind, so I had no reference point for this kind of behavior from a man, other than what I had experienced with my boyfriend from college. I certainly did not expect this behavior from someone who was *in ministry*. However, he began to change for the worst; and the worse he got, the more I ignored the changes, mostly so I could keep the peace within the relationship and be the "good" wife. I learned quickly not to address these concerns dealing with his behavior because any confrontation was upsetting to him.

With each passing day, amidst suspicions of all sorts by me, I tolerated his rage and uncontrollable damaging actions toward me.

Initially, it began with harsh words, put downs, name calling, belittling, and cussing. Behaviors that in my opinion, were not acceptable from a man toward a woman, especially someone, again, who was in ministry. Eventually, these verbal and emotional attacks escalated to his behavior becoming physical against me for no apparent reason. Just being in the room at a certain time or asking a question, resulted in physical attacks against me.

The mistake I made (like most) was to never report the abuse properly to the authorities. Why? These records become public, and again, who wants everyone to know what is going on in their household?

My ex-husband's mindset was that he felt he had the means and financial backing to do whatever he desired thereby covering up his unacceptable behaviors. My mindset was to cover up the unhealthy behaviors by remaining silent. Either way, these types of mindsets negatively teach us and those around us how to cover up for the protection of our *image* and *position.*

People of public prominence and affluence are oftentimes the worst at not reporting abuse to the authorities, while inadvertently, covering up these unacceptable behaviors. This is not healthy for anyone. Typically, even people close to you or in your circle will suspect things, but will not say anything to you because of your position – *more cover up.* If there are children involved, who wants to have these types of things negatively affect their view of a parent? So we think. Listen, children will grow up one day, learn the truth and make their own choices.

The truth? Choices? When our fall from the top happened (or as I like to say our world turned upside down overnight), and as reports of betrayal, adultery, assault and drugs unfolded, years later a number of people told me that they had seen warning signs and had concerns. ***This is a vicious cycle that has to be broken.***

Now that I have grown, healed and matured, I can readily admit that I lived in that place of suffering. I want you to know that even now, for me, it takes much courage and strength to admit this. However, I know this is a necessary process for me and I want to be open and honest about my experience.

I know there might be some people who won't believe my story. Looking over my own story, I too, find it hard to believe that I had allowed this to become my reality. Today, as I look back over my life, it is my hope that many (including you) will relate to my story and make a decision to break the silence and seek help. You see, as I was suffering, I grew numb. I stopped feeling the pain. I covered it up. I tolerated the intolerable to keep peace...SILENCE!

Perhaps, like me, this is your situation. My advice and wisdom to you is that when you see it, ask the Lord to open your eyes fully, so you can begin to **see it** and **say it** in order to break the silence and no longer suffer.

These past seven years, I have been HEALING IN SILENCE. ***This is when the SILENCE is useful and healthy.*** I had to silence the critics, the media, the naysayers, and forgive those that hurt me, turned on me and walked away. In the SILENCE is where I found a place for my soul to enter a state of peace and rest. This place of peace and rest, found in SILENCE, was necessary in order for me to build my inner person, and to clear my thoughts.

Why now am I coming forth? Because I believe this is the appointed time that God has called me to share my story! Over these seven years, I realized that I am one that now has the strength to stand and take this platform.

My seven years of SILENCE have been well spent in the presence of God - *healing, reflecting, resolving, forgiving, rebuilding and coming to a place of peace*!

I want to help you get to that place of peace as well. You must know and believe that you do not have to suffer any longer!

I hope my courage of me BREAKING MY SILENCE helps you to BREAK YOUR SILENCE and BREAK FREE to a new life!

BREAKING FREE – BREAKING THE SILENCE TIP

Exercise: Do You Know Who They Really Are?

We often think that we know people. We must learn to build time-tested relationships to really get to know an individual. During a courtship, we typically all put on our best. If not careful, we cover up or mask our true selves so that our potential partner won't see the "other side" of us. We need to see all sides in courtship before the marriage. When two people desire to marry, each person must submit to wise and proven counsel that is balanced in its approach when dealing with both individuals.

I think the lines often get crossed especially in Christian relationships, so we must learn to proceed with caution and really get to know the person. Beneath all of that makeup, clothes, successful careers, fame and fortune there could be lurking hurt, trauma, pain, anger, and abuse that prevent the relationship from being healthy and whole.

It is my recommendation that you:

- Identify and deal with all issues and resolve them before moving forward.
- Don't listen to what you want to hear, but HEAR what you must know.
- Deal immediately with core root issues "red flags" that are not healthy.
- Find individuals that can "coach" you through this process.

TRUST is the glue of life.
It's the most essential
ingredient in effective
communication.
It's the foundational principle
that holds all relationships.

Adversity is defined as "a condition marked by misfortune, calamity, or distress."

We have all faced adversity; it's what we do to overcome adversity that determines our ability to live again.

Renee Hornbuckle

Chapter 4

EVADING
DANGER SIGNS

Avoiding the Impending Silence

In relationships, everything usually starts out well, but as time passes (and no I can't give you a definitive time), people can begin to change. Early in our relationship, the signs were present. If there was an opposing opinion that I had in a discussion, I was expected to really not express it. Opposing views were seen as not being in support of my partner and seen as non-submissive behavior. This was a challenge for me as an educated, professional woman, but given that I didn't want to upset him, even if I didn't agree or think it was right, I would keep my opinion to myself and just pray. I figured things would change – things would get better.

This type of mindset does not help you in any way. What this does is develop changes in your thought life that create negative learned behaviors over a period of time. Eventually you get to a place where you allow your voice to be silenced and ultimately, silence prevails. You lose your voice – *SILENCE.* Silence causes you to tolerate the intolerable and not speak against the power and control.

Most of us ignore the uneasiness that comes with change, especially negative change. We say things like, "Well, it will get better," or "We can grow out of this, things will change." I do believe that things can and most times do get better, people do mature, and they change. Sometimes (let's be real), it gets worse, people remain stagnant. They change, but for the worse. Depending on what we are taught or what we tolerate, we stay in relationships. We ignore the signs, we become enablers and co-dependent.

So, I don't really know when things really started to dissolve, but apparently somewhere they did. I think at some point I probably even questioned myself and the relationship, but for whatever reason, I ignored the signs.

I believe that it's very important that when two people feel they desire to spend the rest of their lives together that they totally submit to WISE counsel (proven counsel– not people who tell you what you want to hear). Wise counsel that will honestly deal with core root issues that are not healthy. This type of counseling is important because once these issues are dealt with then it allows for each person to become healthy, whole and complete.

You need people in your life that will help you deal with the *real* you, and not the *dating* you. When people help us to see what's beneath the makeup – hurt, pain, anger, abuse, etc., it helps us become whole. If the negative stuff you bring into the relationship is not dealt with, it most likely will come out in the relationship at some point. I believe it is most beneficial to the success of relationships to address the issues immediately.

Again, I believe that in our situation, there were many unresolved issues that were negative factors in both the marriage and ministry. Don't get me wrong, it's actually quite normal to deal with problems in a relationship. However, the important thing is to know how to deal with the major problematic issues that really create major problems, because how you deal with them will determine how your relationship ends up.

You have to look at the relationship as it really is. Ignoring signs and symptoms because you are just caught up in the relationship is not healthy. It will only make it difficult for you to discern or notice things that are not going in the right direction. This is what I did. When you are caught up in the relationship you tend to not properly judge what is said. You ignore harsh words and put downs. You tend to make excuses for negative behaviors. Again, this is the mistake I made.

In looking back over the early years, I have to confess that I was in denial and became uneasy about my relationship. I was not able to openly communicate about my feelings and concerns. Communication was an issue. It was basically one sided. I did as I was told. In attempts to break beyond that barrier, I would write letters, set appointments for us to have heart to heart discussions so that we could confront the issues as they presented themselves. I am one of those people that believe that you need to discuss things to bring resolution. Unfortunately, these efforts to communicate were met with disdain.

Somewhere along the way, as I tried to face and deal with issues, my will to fight lessened and eventually a wall emerged ultimately taking me to a place of denial. The only thing is that once you are in these types of situations they become normal and you begin to simply become numb to the abnormal behaviors and unacceptable treatment.

Heeding To the Warning Signs

Identifying the early danger signs of impending silence consist of many factors.

First, acknowledgement and acceptance of *'life as it is'* is the first step you must take. Coming out of denial and getting understanding of what's really going on is paramount.

You may search yourself and ask specific questions:

- What is really going on?
- What am I accepting?

- What should I truthfully call it? Ex: Control, Isolation, etc.
- How should I label what I am seeing?
- Can I share what I am seeing with someone else without being ashamed?

You see, for a long time I could not and would not call it anything. Why? I could not say the words. My intellectual mind would not let me say what it was. I had justified within my mind that I was **only** experiencing just harshness of words in my relationship. And every now and then, some name-calling or put downs. Surely, I was not experiencing what others called abuse, "Me, an educated, intelligent, successful, happy, loving woman who loved life? Abuse? Really?" I finally thought. "How did I get here? What was going on? What was each danger sign or warning representing?"

As I begin to look at the definition of abuse (I'm a researcher), there were things on the list that I knew I had experienced, but I was too ashamed to admit.

As I looked at the various definitions of abuse deeper, I begin to get understanding. The Bible tells us that Wisdom is the principal thing; therefore get wisdom. And in all your getting, get understanding (Proverbs 4:7 NKJV).

So, as I sought for understanding, I found this definition of domestic violence:

Domestic violence can be defined as a pattern of behavior in any relationship that is used to gain or maintain power and control over an intimate partner.

"A pattern of behavior?" What was this pattern? How was it affecting me?

"Used to gain or maintain power?" Had this been used to strip me of my identity and to gain power over me?

- *"Control...over a partner? "*
- *"Over me?"*
- *"A smart person"?*
- *"A person who knew better?"*

I reflected back on my marriage and I realized that these patterns of behavior had been used in my life by my partner to gain power and control over me, especially the *verbal and mental abuse*.

It is common that victims of *verbal and mental abuse* often fail to perceive the true aggression to which they have been subjected. I felt torn down and belittled most days. The damage of *verbal and mental abuse* is most often to the mental and emotional well-being, barely visible to the naked eye. For someone like me, it's easy to cover up or mask the anguish felt in situations like this. I knew how to encourage myself, and be strong; to hide the tears; the pain. But at the end of each day, I still asked myself, "Is this really abuse?"

Verbal abuse can be more detrimental to your mental health because this becomes what you believe, so it creates confusion in your mind. I dismissed it and told myself, "no". I continued to live in this state of denial - doing so to justify things were okay – telling myself that things would get better. You see, I wasn't being physically hit (yet). All along I knew the verbal, emotional and psychological actions against me were extreme, unhealthy and unchristian like.

As other issues continued to unfold, I researched further and I found the following definitions:

> *Abuse is physical, sexual, emotional, economic or psychological actions or threats of actions that influence another person. This includes any behaviors that frighten, intimidate, terrorize, manipulate, hurt, humiliate, blame, injure or wound someone.*

Domestic violence can happen to anyone of any race, age, sexual orientation, religion or gender. It can happen to couples who are married, living together or who are dating. **Domestic violence** affects people of all socioeconomic backgrounds and education levels.

Had this been what I had been living under all these years? Was I ready to deal with the dysfunction of the relationship? Could I say what it was? Finally, I was forced to say it – ABUSE!

SIGNS AND WARNINGS

There are signs and warnings that usually set off internal alarms and raise red flags. We can't ignore them or pretend like they don't exist. We have to get out of the place of denial and be honest with where we are.

There are often common Sense Signs and Warnings (Alarms) that we should be aware of. I realized I had learned these things growing up, but I had not applied them to my relationship. These are some of the simple principles I learned over my lifetime:

- If it doesn't feel right; it probably isn't right.

- If you think something is wrong; most likely it is.

- If you detect odd and unacceptable behaviors; don't ignore them, the person is showing you who they really are.

- If you witness irrational anger or rage emerges; chances are there are deep rooted issues that need resolve.

- If unrealistic expectations and demands are placed upon you, rarely will they change; expect to live with these false expectations and demands.

- If attitudes are unpredictable and you have to walk on eggshells, chances are the person has a control issue.

- A real man would never lay his hands on a woman or vice versa.

As I reflected upon these life principles, I realized I had not practiced any of them. My wisdom to you is open your eyes and see life as it really is!

Your quality of life depends on it!

BREAKING FREE – BREAK THE SILENCE TIP

Exercise: Understanding Abuse

The Bible tells us, "Wisdom is the principal thing; therefore get wisdom. And in all your getting, get understanding" (Proverbs 4:7).

As I sought wisdom and understanding, I found the following information that can also be of help to you.

Read, respond, and be willing to take action when and if needed. As I said before, no one, and I do mean no one, should have to *suffer in silence*.

Definitions of Abuse:

Domestic violence can be defined as a pattern of behavior in any relationship that is used to gain or maintain power and control over an intimate partner.

Domestic violence can happen to anyone of any race, age, sexual orientation, religion or gender. It can happen to couples who are married, living together or who are dating. Domestic violence affects people of all socioeconomic backgrounds and education levels.

Abuse is physical, sexual, emotional, economic or psychological actions or threats of actions that influence another person. This includes any behaviors that frighten, intimidate, terrorize, manipulate, hurt, humiliate, blame, injure or wound someone.

Breaking Free – Breaking The Silence

Do you think you might be in an abusive relationship?

The next few sections are composed of topical checklists that I obtained from the **National Center on Domestic Violence**. Go through the checklists thoroughly and check all that apply. In performing this exercise, the most important thing for you to do is BE HONEST!

Check those answers that apply:

You may be in an *emotionally abusive* relationship if your partner:

____Calls you names, insults you or continually criticizes you

____Does not trust you and acts jealous or possessive

____Tries to isolate you from family or friends

____Monitors where you go, who you call and who you spend time with

____Does not want you to work

____Controls finances or refuses to share money

____Punishes you by withholding affection

____Expects you to ask permission

____Threatens to hurt you, the children, your family or your pets

____Humiliates you in any way

Check those answers that apply:

You may be in a *physically abusive* relationship if your partner has ever:

___Damaged property when angry (thrown objects, punched walls, kicked doors, etc.)

___Pushed, slapped, bitten, kicked or choked you

___Abandoned you in a dangerous or unfamiliar place

___Scared you by driving recklessly

___Used a weapon to threaten or hurt you

___Forced you to leave your home

___Trapped you in your home or kept you from leaving

___Prevented you from calling police or seeking medical attention

___Hurt your children

___Used physical force in sexual situations

Check those answers that apply:

You may be in a *sexually abusive* relationship if your partner:

___Views women as objects and believes in rigid gender roles

___Accuses you of cheating or is often jealous of your outside relationships

___Wants you to dress in a sexual way

___Insults you in sexual ways or calls you sexual names

___Has ever forced or manipulated you into to having sex or performing sexual acts

___Held you down during sex

___Demanded sex when you were sick, tired or after beating you

___Hurt you with weapons or objects during sex

___Involved other people in sexual activities with you

___Ignored your feelings regarding sex

If you answered "YES" to most of these

questions, you may be in an abusive

relationship; please call the

National Domestic Violence Hotline

at 1-800-799-SAFE (7233),

1-800-787-3224 (TTY),

or your local Domestic Violence Center to talk

with someone about it.

Don't wait – call NOW!

Breaking Free – Breaking the Silence

Exercise: Strengthen your senses to be able to recognize "danger feelings."

In late 1965, the popular show "Lost In Space" came on the scene. The show featured an overgrown robot. When danger approached the family, Robot would scream in a loud voice, "Warning!" so that the family would not be harmed.

In this exercise, I want you to strengthen your senses to be able to recognize "danger feelings."

With our children, most of us taught them "Good Touch, Bad Touch". Maybe you were not taught how to recognize your own "good feelings, bad feelings".

With abusive relationships we lose the ability to recognize when our senses are sending us a warning.

Using your entries from Exercise #1, I want you to look at all the feelings you identified. Now, in this exercise write them down and put a check next to the ones you would consider as "warning feelings".

Do the same for the thoughts you listed in Exercise #1. Go ahead and add any other feelings or thoughts that the Holy Spirit brought to your attention that you did not list in the previous exercise.

Re-read the list and pray to God acknowledging His power to heal your senses to alert you of danger in any relationships.

With our senses restored, we can begin again to trust ourselves and others. If we trust ourselves and others, then we can begin to believe again. You must believe that life is worth living. Your belief will help create and shape your new future.

Bad things do happen; how I respond to them defines my character and the quality of my life. I can choose to sit in perpetual sadness, immobilized by the gravity of my loss, or I can choose to rise from the pain and treasure the most precious gift I have - life itself.

Walter Anderson

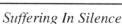

Chapter 5

SILENT CRIES

How Did I Get Here?

"You are clinically depressed," are the words I heard the counselor say to me. Finally, I could not take it anymore. My life and my mind had become so overwhelmed by my husband's expectations and demands that I finally had a mental collapse. I knew something was wrong with me, but I did not know what. But every day I came home from work, immediately, I would walk into the bedroom, crawl into the bed and completely cover my head with the covers. This went on for months.

Me? Depressed? Surely not - a pastor's wife and a successful business woman? Yes! There were so many expectations put on me from my ex-husband that I lost my identity. Expectations whether I wanted to or not, I was to live up to. I was expected to step up and do what he instructed. It was his way of molding me into the model of the perfect ministry wife. When I didn't measure up to his expectations, he started to put me down by making belittling comparisons to successful women in ministry. Eventually, it started to take a toll on me and I begin to lose my identity. I was so busy trying to live up to his expectation of me; wanting nothing more than to be the woman that he desired of me. But that was the problem. I was so busy trying to please my husband that I lost my identity, which caused me to question my value and self-worth, ultimately resulting in depression.

However, I worked diligently to create this person he desired me to be instead of searching for who God designed me to become. I lost myself because of false expectations. Now as I look back, and have become honest with myself, I have to admit the silent cries started many years earlier.

Mentally and emotionally abusive relationships often have few outward symptoms. The Mayo Clinic suggests symptoms of mental abuse include low self-esteem, cutting off contact with loved

115

ones and friends, and inappropriate worry. Individuals who experience emotional abuse or constant putdowns and criticisms often display other signs as well.

Being a strong, independent, successful woman married to a man still searching for his identity and personal success, was another factor that caused early problems within the marriage. I was comfortable with and supported his pursuit of his career and higher education because I knew he had great potential! However, this was something that he continually struggled with and as a result it caused him to constantly be in the mode of feeling he had to prove himself. Nevertheless, his expectations for me to be molded into what he desired ran parallel with his pursuits to prove himself.

As I transitioned into the role of a pastor's wife there were even more challenges. Pastor's wives were typically placed into stereotypical categories with certain expectations. Most were expected to sing or play the piano. I did not do either. I was not a singer or piano player, but a business woman who had dreams of climbing the corporate ladder.

My ex-husband had accepted this, but also wanted me to be in ministry. He would often compare me to women evangelists who were successful and encourage me to step into ministry. He would tell me that he felt I would be great in ministry. I appreciated the encouragement, but deep inside this created internal turmoil for me. I had studied Business in college and enjoyed being in the marketplace climbing the ladder to success. I was comfortable in the board room, but not in the pulpit. It became increasingly apparent that what he desired for me was for me to step into the role as a speaker.

He worked with me to develop my ministry speaking skills, but I still was not truly confident in this arena. But because of my reluctance to step into this role, he began to make comparisons of how great certain women ministers were and how he desired to have a wife that would serve alongside him in ministry in the same capacity. But it was only a matter of time before the encouragement became an expectation. Therefore, I lost myself because of false expectations. But as layers were exposed, the findings of the cause of my depression was loss of identity mainly due to mental and emotional control being inflicted on me, alienated from loved ones and friends, and the constant putdowns; feeling totally inadequate.

Again, here I was faced with how to address this with someone I supposedly loved, but who was controlling. Again, the wrong choice – SILENCE.

When I was diagnosed with being clinically depressed, I did whatever was necessary in order for me to regain my confidence and esteem. Unfortunately, I was still overlooking the causes - the constant putdowns, criticisms of everything I did, separation from family, false expectations, and verbal and emotional abuse. I resolved that it would be easier to do the work that the counselor recommended to 'fix me'. Also, I resolved that I didn't have to say anything to him about what was identified as the cause of my depression.

This resolve brought about silence once again. In my silence, I sought to do the work requested of me. Now, committed to doing the work, after displaying and dealing with the visible systems of depression, I developed extreme stomach ulcers. It was concluded that these stomach ulcers resulted from constant worry, being disconnected from family and friends and personal internal turmoil.

Had all this affected my well-being?
Had I been trapped for years?
Why were these relational issues unresolved?

I dealt with my depression and ultimately overcame it.

In the following year, things did get better as we entered the stage of parenting. We were excited and happy about being new parents and our new additions to the family. God blessed us with a beautiful baby boy and girl 15 months apart. For a period of time, I continued in my corporate position until the weightiness of parenting caused me to make a decision to being a full time, stay-at-home mom. I wish I could say this was something I was ecstatic about; however, I was thankful that we had a lifestyle that afforded me the opportunity to come off my job. But now I was faced with leaving a position that I had worked hard to succeed in, but the decision was made and I became a full time house wife and mother. It, too, was a challenge for me.

Making the transition from corporate climber to stay-at-home mom once again threatened my identity. I finally got the mommy thing down, but the transition into ministry was still what seemed to be an unachievable expectation.

On one occasion, when I was struggling with the transition, my husband desired for me to make into ministry, he strongly encouraged me to attend a conference. In fact, he put me on a plane with my two babies and sent me to Oklahoma. I actually didn't have a choice – the ticket was purchased, so I packed, and was on my way with a one year old and two year old in tow. However, this conference for women really did make a positive impact on me personally and on my view of myself in ministry. In fact, it was in one of the sessions at this conference when I finally realized the main difficulties I had in making the transition into ministry.

One of the main issues I had with being a pastor's wife in full time ministry or any type of speaker was that I didn't fit into a traditional mold. I had blond spiked hair (that later became my signature), wore glamour makeup, wore my skirts a little bit above my knee, and my shoes were quite ornate, jeweled and high. Never had I seen this model of what I was expected to become. I had not seen in ministry a woman that mirrored the type of woman I was. I felt as though I was expected to comply with the code of dress and fit into a certain type of box. I had read in the Bible that women were always beautifully adorned, so I never saw how I being a classy, professional, business woman would be a problem. I had studied women of the Bible and was often enamored by their unique callings and individuality. But as a young pastor's wife, apparently in most religious circles this was taboo; and therefore, the root of my issue.

That day in the meeting, I intentionally sat in the back of the room. This was my way of expressing my contempt and defiance for being there in the first place. Even though I was there, I really didn't want to be there. Soon, the guest speaker for the session, an African American woman, graced the platform to speak. When she stepped forward to the podium, I was looking down. Something caught my eye — a glimmer, a sparkle. As I graciously raised my head, my eye caught the glimmer — the tip of her shoes. The tip of the shoe seemed to reflect so much of me, or who I used to be -- a sparkly, happy person who loved life.

As I raised my head seemingly in slow motion, I carefully examined every piece of garment she had on. It was like an MRI Cat Scan, having the x-ray machine slowly moving up and down the body to scan the entire body from head to toe. Finally, I had seen and found someone who looked like me! I realized in that moment that I didn't have to be bound. I finally had a defining moment that, **"I COULD DO ME."**

This woman was classy and gorgeous. Everything she had on was absolutely stylish — it reflected beauty. Her hair, and definitely her shoes that had snapped me out of my stupor, were unique and unusual, but reflected her beauty. She captured the attention of both me and the audience as she confidently shared the Word of God! After the meeting, I met her and she was so kind and gracious. So for years, after this, I ordered every tape and book that she produced and watched her on television every chance I could. This was such a defining and pivotal moment in my life.

So when I returned home from the conference, I was a brand new Renee! Well, internally I was new. While things had not changed externally, I knew I had changed internally. Rather than admit to my husband that I had experienced the change, I decided the best thing to do was to thank him for sending me to the conference and then show him the change. He did notice and acknowledged the change initially and was excited. I, too, was also excited! I had found a way to meet his expectations. Life was grand!

It Only Lasts For A Short While

Eventually, things went back to the old way. So, now the 'NEW ME', with my renewed confidence of transitioning into ministry, had to deal with the constant putdowns, criticisms of everything I did, separation from family, false expectations, and verbal and emotional abuse again. Here it was again. But this time I felt empowered.

Eventually, I resolved that in my new, empowered state, I would still continue to yearly do all the work that the counselor had recommended years earlier to fix me – a type of tune up. As time went on, I knew I had been "fixed" and that I had changed!

In spite of everything I shall rise again: I will take up my pencil, which I have forsaken in my great discouragement, and I will go on with my drawing.

Vincent Van Gogh

Is your relationship based on power and control?

Physical and sexual assaults, or threats to commit them, are the most apparent forms of domestic violence and are usually the actions that allow others to become aware of the problem. However, regular use of other abusive behaviors by the batterer, when reinforced by one or more acts of physical violence, make up a larger system of abuse. Although physical assaults may occur only once or occasionally, they instill threat of future violent attacks and allow the abuser to take control of the woman's life and circumstances.

The Power & Control diagram is a particularly helpful tool in understanding the overall pattern of abusive and violent behaviors, which are used by a batterer to establish and maintain control over his partner. Very often, one or more violent incidents are accompanied by an array of these other types of abuse. They are less easily identified, yet firmly establish a pattern of intimidation and control in the relationship.

VIOLENCE
PHYSICAL · SEXUAL

Power & Control

COERCION & THREATS
Making and/or carrying out threats to do something to hurt her · threatening to commit suicide or report her to welfare · making her drop charges · making her do illegal things

INTIMIDATION
Making her afraid by using looks, actions, and gestures · smashing things · destroying her property · abusing pets · displaying weapons

EMOTIONAL ABUSE
Putting her down · making her feel bad about herself · calling her names · making her think she's crazy · playing mind games · humiliating her · making her feel guilty

ISOLATION
Controlling what she does, who she sees and talks to, what she reads and where she goes · limiting her outside involvement · using jealousy to justify actions

MINIMIZING, DENYING, & BLAMING
Making light of the abuse and not taking her concerns about it seriously · saying the abuse didn't happen · shifting responsibility for abusive behavior · saying she caused it

USING CHILDREN
Making her feel guilty about the children by telling her she is a bad parent or by telling her the children need a two-parent home · threatening to hurt the children · using the children to relay messages · using visitation to harass her · threatening to take the children away

ECONOMIC ABUSE
Preventing her from getting or keeping a job · making her ask for money · giving her an allowance · taking her money · not letting her know about or have access to family income

MALE PRIVILEGE
Treating her like a servant · making all the big decisions · acting like the 'master of the castle' · being the one to define men's and women's roles

PHYSICAL · SEXUAL
VIOLENCE

Taken from:

Texas Council on Family Violence

Chapter 6

SILENT ANGISH

Coping with Catastrophe, Loss and Denial

I couldn't wait to turn 40! The age of maturity, the next chapter! I embraced life.

However, when my husband and I turned 40, things really intensify and began to spiral out of control. Like any good Christian wife, I prayed. The reality was that he needed help. At first, it was just little things he did that were odd and not of good Christian character, but I figured that he would get through it in time and we would move forward. In fact, I found myself making excuses and justifying my husband's behavior. But as time passed, his behavior got even odder. Any questioning him brought unpleasant confrontation, harsh words and demeaning responses. Most times, I just looked the other way, ignored it, and managed life--children, ministry and business.

The things that brought me pleasure, happiness and success actually consumed most of my time. I had convinced myself that in spite of the occasional mood swings and demands from my husband, life was wonderful! So I would find things that made life enjoyable.

In spite of everything, I really loved taking care of my husband, family and home. I enjoyed serving in ministry and being an entrepreneur. Now, with three active, energetic children, I was always there to support them in their endeavors. I was traveling more, and the ministry and business grew more demanding also.

As I got busier, so did my husband. The times that we spent away from each other would easily allow a person to freely have opportunity for other activities. One of the things I learned early in life was to trust people until they proved otherwise. Therefore, I didn't question his comings and goings. If he said he was to be someplace, I trusted him. And given that I was not a hovering wife, the usual questioning of whereabouts, phone calls, odd behaviors, suspicious schedules and times, were not information I sought. It wasn't until his behavior really took on extremes that disrupted our personal, family and church life that I grew remotely concerned.

Reality hit...

When we were faced with lawsuits and reports in the media, unbelievable stories of drugs, betrayal and multiple adulterous affairs is when reality hit me "square in the face." Initially, it didn't make sense. I really did try to support his reasoning for the horrific attacks we were facing. We had achieved much in life, and we knew there would be people trying to pull us down.

As things began to unravel and the year progressed after the initial alleged report, it was apparent that something was definitely wrong. Our life and the daily pressures we faced each day became incredibly overwhelming. As soon as I tried to catch my breath, more accusations would unfold. It was really crazy for me, my children, and for the ministry. It was absolutely overwhelming!

Still not being able to prove anything, but having suspicion of something being wrong, I remember crying out to God and saying, "God, I don't know what's happening, BUT like JOB...I will trust YOU!" I finally got to the place where I was forced out of my state of denial.

When one is in denial, eventually, there comes a time when you have to make a choice to open your eyes, look at the situation for what it is and either come out of that denial or continue to live in denial. Finally, something snapped me out of the denial. I began to look around and see that there were so many that were affected by the adverse actions of the man who I called my husband.

Once I came out of denial, God allowed me to see the situation from the various perspectives. Literally, overnight, our world as we (me, children, family, church family) knew it fell apart! This was an extremely hurtful place to be. It hurt. It was devastating! It was painful.

Everything we knew had been pulled out from underneath us. It was like being beat up and left for dead. It took me a few minutes to regroup. I had to get up because too many people were affected and needed comforting. The media was around, stuff was on the news, and it was printed in the paper (the media for a period of time was in the church every service and often on the sidewalk across the street from both my house and church). I had to take my children to school while all this was going on...I mean it was totally shocking! Absolutely crushing!

As things continued to fall apart rapidly, I did the best that I could to make it through each day. I lived in this state of chaos for well over a year. Finally, as my husband's court day approached, I found myself alone with God, and totally depending on Him.

By this time, I had learned to take each day as it came. That's all I often had strength to do. Now, here I was, sitting in a criminal courtroom. Almost a month was spent in courtrooms. The things I heard in the courtroom were astounding and I could not believe the things that were presented by each side. I thought to myself, "This man has led a double life. I don't know this person. I can't believe he lied to me!" Witness after witness was called to the stand to give testimony. After all I had invested in this man and this marriage, I realized the man I thought I knew; I didn't know at all! I was living with a stranger. "What happened to the person I married? Who in the world did I marry? What had happened?" I thought.

It was obvious that things were greatly wrong. That somewhere along the way he became intoxicated with his own success. The emotional, verbal, mental and physical abuse I had experienced had been experienced by others also in so many ways.

Many experienced the betrayal, the manipulation, the control, the selfishness, the abuse of influence and power, the feeding of an unhealthy ego, and the narcissism. Moreover, here we were sitting in a criminal courtroom with media everywhere. We were sitting here because of one man's extreme selfishness, greed, pride and no self control. My family, other lives and families, our ministry, and our children all embarrassed, humiliated, angry and in emotional and financial ruin because of the abuse of one man.

For those that might ask, "Well, what was your part?" I will accept my responsibility. I got caught up in our life. The ideal couple! The wonderful life of affluence and grandeur! The appearance of the perfect family! Living in a wonderful world, yet, as reality set in, that world was turning into a nightmare. The truth of the matter was that what had become my way of life, I never thought would affect others. What I had been subjected to, I never thought would impact other lives. What I had been in denial about like most, I figured would remain family secrets. I never thought and did not see any hurt or harm coming to others. Yet, I now admittedly can say that I ignored the danger signs, so here yet again, in denial...again, choosing to remain SILENT. This time, SILENT to that which I didn't know, understand or refused to open my eyes to see.

Everything was affected and our life lost what we considered to be normal! In fact, I lost sight of what "NORMAL" was supposed to resemble. I had to get it together. To make certain I could keep it together for me, my children, and those that were looking to me for strength, I pulled on the only person I could trust! GOD!!! Suddenly scripture came to life.

I had to live it! I chose to look for strength that comes from God. I confess that living the scripture is tough to do when you are going through crisis. But in my situation, I recognized that this was too much for me to bear. So I found

Psalm 55:22 (I think I stumbled across it one day when I was under extreme pressure) one day. I read this verse over and over again. *"Cast your cares on the Lord and he will sustain you; He will never let the righteous fall."* I knew this scripture and had used it and preached it often. On this day, it took on new meaning. At this point, I figured I had nothing left to lose, and I didn't really know what else to do. I needed peace in the midst of this mess my life had become. I took the children to school, came home, spent time crying out to God for help and studying the Word of God. I was desperate for answers, but more so needed to be at peace and be comforted! What I found in my study was that the word 'cast' in Greek means to throw it away. Throw your pain, your disappointment, your broken dreams, and your heart ache onto the Lord, for He cares for you.

I said out loud, "Lord, this is a good time to see if you really care for me? And if you consider me righteous I know you won't let me fall any further than I have. Right?" I can remember thinking to myself, "God, I really can't handle this so I willingly give this crisis to you right NOW!!!" In that moment of weeping, I gladly threw this chaos in my life to the Lord for Him to handle!!!

It was a tough time, and it was hard. Nonetheless, I knew I had to either rise above it, or I knew I would give into it. I had been down before and I didn't like that option. I made a decision. Rather than asking God, "WHY in the world is this happening?" I simply wanted to know HOW this was going to be used for HIS GLORY and for GOOD. I wanted to know what I was supposed to learn and do!!

In Valorie Burton's book, *Listen to Your Life,* she explains it this way:

> *"By virtue of life's tendency to throw curve balls from time to time, you need to be prepared to adjust your priorities so that you will experience the best that life has to offer you, even in the midst of challenging times. At various points certain aspects of your life will require more attention than others. Without an awareness that priorities are ever-changing rather than constant, you'll find yourself struggling to deal with new responsibilities, opportunities, and issues that come into your life."*

She goes on to share how we must learn how to navigate through difficult times in our lives through the mechanism of what she calls, "Flow" -- learning to ride the waves of life's adversities from a positive and an awareness standpoint. And she says the way to determine whether you are moving properly with the rhythm of life that your current life has dealt you is what you ask in challenging times.

She said if you ask, "Why me?" then you are going against the flow of life. Rather you should ask what is this or that experience telling or teaching me? When you learn to go with the flow of life, you are able to handle more in your life – whether good opportunities or bad news. By doing this, you increase your capacity to deal with whatever life may send your way. In addition, she says, *"In the midst of life's difficulties, you connect even more deeply with God, yourself, and others to find comfort, peace, and wisdom."* This is exactly the route my life eventually took on to sustain me through all of this.

From seeking and asking God for guidance, I learned that HE wanted me to be a representative of HIM during this ordeal. To be honest with you, it was not what I wanted to hear. Furthermore, it was not comforting at the time. But if you ever really need something to cause you to get your act together, talk to God, then listen and do what HE tells you. I heard the Lord say loud and clear, "The world will know ME (GOD) through what they see you do, as you walk this out!!! You will become real, visual HOPE for many! You will show others that crisis doesn't have to stop LIFE! You will show them how to make it through crisis and still have an abundant LIFE!"

As a public figure, high-profile individual, influential person or whatever phrase you choose to use, one thing I was clear on, I had a responsibility that I was NOT going to bring additional disgrace and dishonor to God or the

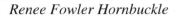

church. I had to represent the KINGDOM of GOD!!! I knew I had to be a righteous voice. We say all the time, "What would Jesus do?" I really had to consider what Jesus would do, especially when the human part of me wanted to both fall apart and retaliate!

As I started on this journey, I had to take a good hard look at myself. I asked myself some sobering questions. "How did I get trapped? Why did I stay?" Why do others get trapped? Why do they stay?

The following is the list that I came up with of how we get trapped and why we stay.

HOW WE GET TRAPPED AND WHY WE STAY

- We simply get caught up in the relationship because we are in love
- Loving the other person more than yourself
- Feeling like we can't make it without them in your life
- Have not overcome your personal short comings
- To save face
- False Christian belief and expectations
- To protect our Image
- Because of the shame and embarrassment
- To keep peace
- For the children. Thinking what will happen to your children without the other parent
- Nowhere to go

- We really do believe they will change
- Don't believe we deserve better
- Fear of the unknown
- Fear of being alone
- Embarrassment of having made wrong choices
- Fear of failure
- Your identity is wrapped up in the other person
- Loss of self esteem
- Sometimes it's just hard to believe that you are in something so bad and tragic!!
- Operating in a co-dependency and enabling
- Looking for the wrong kind of love
- See all acceptance and any kind of abuse as love

So if you get caught up, then how do you get out of it?

HOW DO YOU GET OUT?

You begin to get out by acknowledging the following (check the ones you will commit to work toward):

- It takes courage
- It takes being honest with yourself
- It takes coming to the realization that this is not the life you are supposed to live
- It takes you saying "No", and knowing how and when to set boundaries and where you draw your line
- It takes you knowing when to get out when boundaries are not respected
- It takes a plan

- It takes a support network
- It takes wise counsel – consult your clergy, licensed professionals or domestic violence agency
- It takes strength of mind

Harville Hendrix in his book, *Getting the Love you Want: A Guide for Couples,* urges married people to stay together to work out their issues. This approach to marriage counseling believes that your partner is the right person to help you heal your childhood wounds. With this approach, many marriages can be saved if both partners are willing to do the work required. However, Hendrix says there are three reasons to leave a relationship: ***The Three A's--There are severe abuse, severe adultery and severe addictions***. **These three extreme conditions rarely change.**

For singles, if you see any pending danger signs before you are married make sure you discuss them, confront them, and see change. Also, you must understand that these behaviors most likely will not change *without* the person getting help.

Change is prompted by people who want it and decide to make it happen. You need the right kind of support to make positive change in your life. Find spiritual support, family support and authentic friends who will support you through your transition. And if there is danger, you will need to find the right type of agency to assist you in the transition.

BREAKING FREE – BREAK THE SILENCE TIP

- Make an honest assessment of your situation.

- Look at the history of the person. It's been proven that abused people, if not healed, will abuse people.

- Trust another person or professional to tell them about the abuse. There is safety in the counsel of many. Seek Counsel (legal and spiritual)

- If you are in a violent situation – leave, even if it means leaving everything

- If you don't have finances, contact local agencies.

150

- You must have a plan.

- You must believe that you can get your life back.

- You must believe that you can put the pieces back together.

- It's with God and wisdom that you can find your strength and recapture your joy.

*Courage is doing what
you're afraid to do. There
can be no courage unless
you're scared.*

Eddie Rickenbacker

Chapter 7

EXPOSING

SILENT ISSUES

Breaking the Silence: Getting Help
Getting Beyond Stigmas and Shame

"**H**i, this is Renee Hornbuckle. I'm leaving Terry, so the kids and I are leaving to an undisclosed location. I've got cash so you won't be able to trace me. The keys to our house are in the

153

mailbox. He needs an intervention. I don't really know what's wrong – but I know SOMETHING is wrong. His behavior is strange. He gets upset when I try to confront him and he doesn't want to be held accountable. I will contact you in three days to see if you have helped him. After you do so…I will return," is the script I would rehearse repeatedly in my mind many nights, while my husband was out *most* nights late.

Night after night, I would scroll through my cell phone contact list looking at the private numbers of some of the most powerful men in the country, yet, I never made a single call. With our busy lives, and a plethora of people around me and playing the role so well, very few knew that each night after putting the children to bed that I would spend endless nights alone. So, as my husband's odd behavior intensified in the latter years of our marriage (even though I was married), I often felt alone. I would hold the cell phone in my hand trying to figure out who I should call. Who could help me confront the abnormal behaviors and schedules from a man who was a perceived as a powerful public figure? Who would believe that this leader, husband, and father who projected a "perfect" life had the potential of dark, deviant behaviors?

Where would I turn to? Who would I turn to? Those lonely nights, I sat in bed scrolling through my cell phone, rehearsing that script; yet, never making the call; perhaps, fearful or more so still in denial. Or maybe, I just I never made the call, hoping that things might change.

SILENT...yet again.

Night after night, this scenario played out. He would call every thirty minutes or so to see if I were asleep. Of course, I wasn't asleep because of the continual calls that awakened me if I had dozed off. Fearful of questioning his whereabouts, I would simply ask, "When will you be home?" His reply always the same, "See you in thirty minutes. I love you." Hours would pass; yet, still no husband walking through the door. Often my children would wake up and ask, "Where is Daddy?" I would cover and say, "He will be home soon; I love you, go back to bed." *We both needed help.*

SILENT once again!

On one occasion, we did go to counseling, but I had learned to be silent because of fear. I was not honest. So it caused me to put a mask on and hide.

In counseling I was SILENT, too.

When you live with someone who has the potential for abuse, you tend to remain silent even when help is present. Even though I wanted to tell the truth, I knew the end result of what might occur if I told the truth or exposed him. Again, the anguish of the silence that you learn in order to keep peace has a way of numbing you to reality.

It's the manipulation and control that has a grip on you. You respond in the manner that is expected of you. I had been made to believe that somehow things were *my fault* and *that I needed to do things differently.* Again, as a well-educated, studious, successful woman, I struggled to wrap my mind around this accusation from my husband. Me? My fault? I begin to rehearse in my mind the kind of wife I had been, and while not perfect, I knew in my heart, that I had given all that I had to give to him. I had made it my personal goal in life to be a supportive, loving wife and mother.

I recall on several occasions being asked by him to give up all the things that God had given me in my success: my business; my women's ministry; my travels – all to prove my love.

It seemed as though at one point in my life, everything I touched, "turned to gold." One of the prominent organizations I founded was Women of Influence, Incorporation. Annually, I would host a conference and ladies would travel from near and far to have a "Women of Influence" Personal Development experience. Thousands of women would attend this conference. We had major corporate sponsorships and support. Some of our sponsors were so gracious that we were able to give away elaborate gifts such as diamond bracelets for drawing and gifts. It was truly an empowering encounter. The goal was to empower women to walk in their purpose with boldness and confidence. And to go home with life-changing tools that they could immediately put to use!

My success continued and the demand for my speaking services increased. My Women of Influence non-profit organization even purchased a transitional home, ironically with the mission of "A Place to Heal While Things Get Better." A place of transition offered to women that were not eligible for typical government services. A place of healing designed, for example, for a professional woman going through a divorce, with two children, who lost everything, yet her income did not qualify her to receive services. With no family nearby and nowhere to live what was she to do? There was no place like this available. We were able to make this happen.

However, with all the notoriety that I was achieving, beneath all the grandeur of our public success, the underlining unhealthy personal current in our relationship was evolving. So, he asked me to let go of everything to prove my love. This definitely caused me to open my eyes and question that something was wrong. So, painstakingly, in keeping with being a "good wife," I released those things as he requested. To no avail, it was not enough. There was always more required of me.

By now, I should have seen the red flags. In fact, everything that I now was experiencing should have been red flags for me.

I was definitely in denial.

Denial is something that vividly exists in relationships that are unhealthy. Denial will cause you to not see your present life as reality and operate in a fantasy world; when really all it is- is fiction.

You must be open about the reality of your relationships *and* when people begin to have expectations of you that seem unrealistic, which God doesn't require of you, it is definitely a sign that something is out of balance.

Exposing Silent Issues

The silent issues that we hide are not at all healthy. I knew both from common sense and from ministering to others that unhealthy silent issues needed to be confronted and exposed.

I knew better!

I knew it was not healthy to keep secrets or cover up your partner's anger, abuse or addictions.

I knew unresolved issues could escalate to bigger issues and manifest in dangerous actions.

I knew it was not healthy if your partner expected you to isolate yourself from others, meet every demand, read his or her mind and always give him or her what was expected.

I knew it was unhealthy to not have agreed upon boundaries in the relationship.

I knew it was unhealthy to not draw the line and speak up when things were obviously unhealthy.

I knew it was unhealthy to ignore signs of emotional blackmail, control, manipulation, fear and guilt imposed by a partner intended to keep you silent, keeping you in your suffering.

Even *knowing better* and *knowing* that all of this was unhealthy, I like so many, still fell prey to the trap. I allowed these unhealthy symptoms to rule my life. Unfortunately like many when faced with **any** type of abuse, I have to admit that I remained silent – even though *I knew better*!

Why do we not expose these silent issues in our lives?

For me, it was fear, shame, and embarrassment. I should not be here? I'm smarter than this? I know better? This will cause our lives to topple over? **I endured verbal, emotional and mental**

abuse, and physical abuse. Initially, I tried to minimize the physical abuse.

*Bottom line, **ABUSE IS ABUSE!***

Even the phrase "abusive relationship" was something I would try to dismiss from my mind. Why? Because we usually think of abuse in relationships associated with extreme images of physical abuse such as hitting, kicking and broken bones. But emotional abuse or psychological and emotional dominance and control of one partner over another is still abuse.

Emotional or mental abuse is often less obvious than physical abuse, therefore, people in emotionally abusive relationships often do not realize they are being abused until the abuse has escalated to intense levels.

Even with this knowledge, I could not press myself to break the silence. What would people think? It wasn't about what people thought about me, as much as I believed it would derail their spirituality. For God's sake, we were leaders! We had to set an example! We were depicted as having the all American life – wonderful marriage, great children, the home, the cars and all the other material things that many hoped for. We were not selfish, so we had taught others how to put God first and live the American Dream-to set family as a priority; to honor your marriage; to excel in your life; to do things right, but in actuality, *he* had stopped doing these things.

I believed and **still do believe** everything we taught. I continued to practice the principles we taught in spite of his actions. But there was this one area of darkness with my husband that had to be confronted. This dark side had put us here in this mess of a situation. A mess that I could not grasp fully nor did I have full understanding, yet, I knew that something" was wrong mostly because of the reactions experienced and witnessed each day that were a result of my husband's abnormal thinking, feeling, behaviors and unrealistic demands in situations. The most exhausting behavior I encountered daily was how he would give ultimatums such as telling you to do things entirely his way or else. It was the "or else" that had me fearful.

I knew God did not want me to walk around fearful. Yet, here I was, fearful of what this man might do and of what people would say and think. I was fearful of whatever I believed at the moment - which I had justified in my mind. In fear is never how God wants any of us to live our lives!!!

The fear, shame and pain I felt caused me to keep silent in order to protect my children, family and others around me. The crazy thing about life is that even though you know at the time that things are not right, nor do they make sense, you will go to no ends to protect those around you. I felt as though I had to protect all those around us. I knew that peoples' lives would be affected if I broke my silence and that deeply troubled me. I was perplexed and in a hard place.

My concern was not about protecting me as much as it was about protecting everyone else. I genuinely didn't want people to give up on God. I didn't want my children to be affected by the stigma of being a dysfunctional family or be ashamed. I didn't want my family to become a statistic. I didn't want to fail God! Because I tried to stay knowledgeable of statistics, I also knew that children exposed to any type of abuse or domestic violence at home would suffer symptoms of trauma.

I read that children, especially males, were more likely to intervene when they witnessed any sort of violence (verbal, emotional or physical) from one parent against the other parent – which would then place the child at greater risk for injury or even death. That created an even greater innate need to protect my boys. I also wasn't willing to expose our children to his verbal or physical abuse for fear of the effects on them. They were innocent children and we were supposed to be mature adults – surely we could work through this. I believed things could change.

I was playing a role that was detrimental. Living what appeared to be a grand life, yet in denial of the serious issues within the relationship. Maybe during those years is why I taught so firmly on having the mental and emotional fortitude to overcome challenging experiences. The truth is I never would have advised any other woman to stay in an abusive relationship. The deception entangled me and brought the fear that paralyzed me in this unhealthy relationship. Still, I ignored the issues, turned my head, and prayed things would change. Did they change, like I said earlier, BUT for the worst!

Finally, I realized how detrimental and extremely dangerous things had become. On one occasion with a house full of people, I walked in our bathroom only to be backhanded and knocked into a tub full of water. I had just walked in from preaching and was fully dressed, hair and makeup done. Now, I was soaking wet! I remember thinking, "Thank God there was water in the tub!" I can't imagine what would have happened had my head hit the side of the tub! I thought to myself, "Oh My God! This is enough!" His reason, he felt I had disclosed his behavior and personal business to some of his accountability partners. Actually, I had not spoken with anyone. He was paranoid. The emotional and verbal abuse had finally reached its intensity and the physical abuse manifested! After the incident occurred, he quickly dressed, left our room, and with his usual charismatic humor made excuses for me to our guests and children. Still again, I remained Silent!

On yet another occasion, my ex-husband was highly agitated and things grew progressively worse as the evening progressed. I avoided direct contact with him as I followed our family bedtime rituals with the children. After putting the children to bed, I would spend typically about an hour preparing the children for the next school day and picking up around the house. On this night, I spent about two hours. As I began to prepare myself to retire for the evening, he verbally attacked me with a barrage of questions. He became extremely angry and I ignored him. He viewed anyone ignoring him as a sign of disrespect and for the next hour I had to attentively listen to his ranting and raving. In my mind, I was engaged in prayer! I was praying to be rescued, "Dear God! How do I get out of this?" So, I thought maybe if I leave the house for a little while, maybe he would calm down.

I went to a friend's apartment thinking that surely I would be safe there and could find a few moments to collect myself. Since no one else was at our home that could stay with the children and because he was under house arrest at this time and not permitted to leave the house without permission, I did not think he would follow me. But he did. He came to the door yelling for them to open the door. This friend did not know what was going on and had utmost respect for both of us. But all of that was soon about to change. He did not try to hide his anger. It was like he felt that he had control of them also.

He came in screaming. When he entered the apartment, I was in the restroom. I heard his yelling, which suddenly got closer and closer. I began to really get concerned. "Does he think he is above the law and can do whatever he wants? He must really think he is superior or infallible?" I realized that this was now a major problem. This night would be different; I was going to have to fight back. I recall my friend saying to him, "This is not the way this needs to be handled." She tried to explain to him that I was using the restroom because I was not feeling well. He shoved her out of the way and accused her of lying. My friend quickly responded and lodged her body in front of him and said sternly, "I said, let her finish using the restroom." I was sitting trying to collect my thoughts, when he burst in, lunged toward me and accused me of leaving him and the children, along with some other accusations that were not true nor did they make sense. When I tried to explain that I needed some space, he began to push me. I was surprised by his rage because I believed that he would not antagonize me in the presence of others. I assumed that he would act differently in the home of someone else. Was I wrong!

My friend's home was lavishly decorated, and I caught sight of a large brass candlestick. I remember thinking to myself, that if he came toward me again, I would hit him with it. Quickly grabbing the candlestick, I raised it above my head, but then I lowered it. I realized in that moment that if I hit him with it that it might kill him. Something said, "Put it down. Your children don't need to lose two parents." All I could think of was me killing him and me going to jail. I dropped the candle stick and ran out of the room toward the stairs. I ran to go up the stairs, but he was close behind. He caught my leg and pulled me down the stairs. By now, my other friend had awakened and now ran out of her bedroom. They both yelled at him to stop and tried to tell him that this had gone too far. As he pulled me down the stairs kicking and screaming, my head hitting each step. All I could think about was what am I going to do now.

At this point, it was apparent that he did not care who knew about his actions. I remember him suddenly being sorrowful and tearfully telling them that he would not touch me again. Just as quickly as he attacked me, he began to justify his behavior. He expressed to them that he was just so upset about me lying to him. I remember him raving to them, "Now you see how she acts and treats me. I told you she was not a good and submissive wife." Without even stopping to take a breath, he switched to say, "I am a good person. I didn't mean to hurt her, but all this was her fault." People like this can't see that they have a problem; it's always somebody else who has the problem and needs to change.

My friends were in shock. They knew what they had just witnessed. The look on their faces was more than I could handle. All I could think about was what I would say to them the next time I saw them. Embarrassed and humiliated, I shifted back into my protective mode. I did not want them to get involved or get hurt trying to help me. So I agreed to leave and go back home. I was still trying to care for and protect others.

After the incident, my friends and I did not discuss it any further. Believe it or not, they really did not know what to say because I did not give them an open door to get involved. I again allowed SILENCE to prevail. And this time I saw the effects that SILENCE made on others.

As I look back, I can see that his actions were obviously a result of his abuse of prescriptive medications and illegal drugs. However, at this moment I was still in the dark of all his undertakings. I would say to him that I felt like he was living a double life, only to be accused of making stuff up and being called crazy. And being told that I needed to have my head examined! Even when he was caught in contradictions, he would deny ever saying the first thing, though it may literally have been only seconds since he made the remark. He would say, "Really, how could you think I'd ever have said **that**? "

I realized enough to know that things were officially spiraling out of control. As he continued in this downward spiral things got more volatile; behaviors more irrational. I realize now, he was in a critical place as his spending, his justifications, his excuses, his paranoia, and his lies grew more and more extreme. Not confident in whom I could call upon to find the help and support needed, I remained silent.

So again SILENCE besieged me.

What was I protecting? The image? My Reputation? Saving face? It's astounding to me, that this had actually become part of the life I was living. God had blessed us with a wonderful life (so abuse couldn't be possible). Right? These things were only happening once in awhile (that's the lie the enemy tells you). Right? These occurrences were just responses to pressures he was under and surely this behavior would change (you always try to justify their unacceptable behaviors).

In retrospect, he had shown these same signs and warnings from the very beginning. Maybe not the physical part, but the manipulation, the control and the put downs were evident. Amidst the emotional and mental abuse of constant, damaging put downs and being made to feel as if I were worthless, he still would turn around immediately and say, "I love you." Was this normal? Was I in danger? Were these warning signs? All signs from the beginning. Maybe it was all in my mind, or maybe it was real?

There was never any reasoning with him. It was if he lived in a fantasy that evolved around him. Something had to change. Something had to be done. Why couldn't I find a process of exposing these issues? Why didn't I feel I could go to someone who would listen?

Well, finally I did go to someone and they just told me to pray. Unfortunately, that was not helpful. You see, I had done all that before. So I left feeling that I still needed to take ACTION! I really needed help from someone who would really give me sound counsel and truly help. Since no one seemed to want to be bothered or get involved, I turned to GOD.

BREAKING FREE – BREAK THE SILENCE TIP

EXERCISE: Chapter 7: Exposing Silent Issues

Exposing your own fear, shame and guilt issues is paramount to your recovery. It is helpful to identify all areas of your life where there is fear, shame and guilt.

The other feelings of fear you might have had are: overlooked, petrified, unimportant, dreadful, alone, lonely, trapped. Other feelings for shame include: embarrassed, dishonored, humiliated, and disgraced.

Guilt feelings include remorseful, irresponsible, stupid, and dumb.

Areas of your life to self-examine include, professional, family, physical, educational, social, spiritual and economical.

An "I" statement is a component of assertive communication that allows you, as an individual, to take responsibility for your thoughts and emotions. This type of communication skill discourages you from placing blame on an outside person or event.

"I" Statements consist of a description of how you feel, an indication of the conditions under which you feel that way, and why those conditions cause your emotions. "I" Statements take this form: "**I feel**... *(State your **emotion**)* **when you**.... *(describe their **behavior** or under what conditions you feel this way)* **because**... *(explain **why** their behavior or the conditions cause you to feel this way)*.

Use the "I" statement model below to help you expose your silent issues and rethink your options. I have included a brief sample to get you started.

Model: I feel (name *your fear, shame, or guilt feeling*) when (*briefly describe the event*).

Example: I feel <u>fearful</u> when <u>I'm all alone and without help.</u>

Model: When I think (a positive trait or thought) and I feel (positive trait) I will (the action you will take).

Example: When I think <u>my life is important</u> and I feel <u>empowered</u> I will <u>call 911.</u>

<u>*Now it's your turn for YOU to take responsibility for your thoughts and emotions so that the silent (hidden) issues can be exposed and you can begin to rethink your options!*</u>

If you're thinking about ending an abusive relationship, but you're not sure where to turn, you can get free, anonymous support and advice from the **National Domestic Violence Hotline or reference information in the appendix**.

Remember, if you see the warning signs, get help!

And also remember, healing from a controlling, mentally abusive relationship takes time, effort, support, patience and prayer.

Chapter 8

BREAKING

THE SILENCE

When Leaving Is the Only Option

"I AM A MAD WOMAN ON EDGE," I shouted while in a heated argument with my husband. By this time in our marriage, I had gained the strength and stamina to fight back. I came to grips that I really was not the bad or terrible person I was told I was for so many years. But after this argument, I knew something had to change. But regardless of all of this, I so desperately still wanted my marriage to work. When I read the book by Harville Hendrix, *Getting the Love You Want: A Guide for Couples*, I thought to myself surely I can find a way to turn all of this around. I even recall thinking, maybe he's just going through a mid-life crisis...here I was again making excuses for his behavior. I continued to read the guide book by Hendrix.

After reading Hendrix's book, I started to confront my husband more, each time resulting in more physical abuse. Over the final year, I began to take off my blinders, open my eyes and see what was going on. He had grown lax in how he handled things. There were suspicious phone calls, people, behaviors and habits that began to set off alarms within me. Finally, I gained the strength and began to fight back.

I told God, as I began to open my eyes more and more, "God, I KNOW things are wrong. This needs to stop. I can't seem to get any solid evidence of what he is doing. One of us will have to go, if not, the next time I fight back, one of us will get hurt."

On one occasion, I actually fled the house. He claimed I ran over him. I didn't. I told him to get out of my way and well, the car brushed against him. I was gone for days. I was able to get cash (I couldn't risk using any credit cards because he could track me) and stayed at a hotel. I had to trust that my children would be fine. I knew this time I had to go or someone would really get hurt. When I returned days later, that's when things got progressively worse. Even in the midst of all of this, I remained silent. I said nothing-- unwaveringly, trying to protect the image. Or so I told myself, the embarrassment for the children, the church, and the family. The biggest mistake I made, like so many, never reporting any of this to the authorities.

It just seemed like playing the role was easier, even when I knew the best thing to do was leave. Apparently, this progression of SILENCE was now a part of my daily role playing.

Finally, the police came to the house to make their final arrest after he had once again violated the law.

My husband was arrested on that day for a final time with no opportunity to make bail; I believe that was God's way of **helping me leave,** since I appeared unable to make the decision to do so.

It was over. He was gone. He had been forced to leave. In spite of it all, I believe God got me out. I had been freed from the suffering. It's hard to explain. It brought much relief and peace. **I HAD FINALLY LEFT.**

Every reason Hendrix said in his book why a person should leave a toxic relationship, I experienced it. Now, out of the relationship, people felt I was still silent. Yes, I was SILENT. That is true. But I was SILENT to those seeking details of this drama; SILENT to the media; and SILENT to trying to explain what had happened. *It is a difficult thing to try to give voice to something that you really don't know.* The best thing to do when you don't know is to be silent. And it is in **this silence,** in this stillness, that you can begin to gain insight on how to overcome and move forward with your life

SILENCE
is the sleep that nourishes
wisdom.

Francis Bacon

BREAKING FREE – BREAK THE SILENCE TIP

When Leaving is the Only Option

If you are still vacillating between thoughts and ideas on how to begin the process of leaving, here are some steps you might want to consider:

A. Have you weighed the danger of the relationship, so your plan will succeed in leaving?

B. Have you viewed the seriousness of the threat?

C. Will the children be safe with your mate, boyfriend or father?

If you must leave, reference the Safety Planning Guide in the Appendix on how to leave.

YOU MUST HAVE A PLAN!

*God grant me the serenity to
accept the things I cannot
change, the courage to change
the things I can, and the wisdom
to know the difference.*

Reinhold Niebuhr

Chapter 9

CHANGE

Overcoming Silence & Moving Forward

This is it. The first day of the trial had finally arrived. I drove into the courthouse parking garage, met my friends and family, and proceeded to walk the one block journey to the courthouse. As I left the parking garage and entered the public sidewalk, I could see the media and others already gathered awaiting my appearance. As I made my way up the courthouse steps, cameras were shoved into my face as reporters were screaming questions one after another toward me. They disassembled as I made my way through security and up the elevator only to be once again met by another group of cameras and reporters as the elevator doors opened. I made my way through the crowds to find a seat in the courthouse corridor outside the assigned courtroom, with the media watching my every move, often reading my lips, looking for my expressions.

My husband's attorneys would meet me outside the courtroom and as we huddled for last minute details, they would spew protocol instructions to me and encouraged me not to respond to what might be presented in court. Because the media was always within listening distance, everything had to be done in a non-descript manner, devoid of any facial expressions or gestures. We were instructed where to be seated, and coached on courtroom protocol. As they were giving last minute legal defense strategies, I had reservations and concerns. I found that this was not an experience that I had ever envisioned in my life. The harsh realities of this entire situation seemed so surreal.

You see, from the time my husband was allegedly accused of doing all these outrageous things, even up until the court date, I had gone through a lot more hell in the background that most people were not aware of. Many decisions had to be made regarding our lives, our children's life, our church affairs and our finances. Mentally, physically and financially, we were drained and depleted. I can't begin to tell you of the many days and nights the difficulty in simply getting out of my bed to face another day or falling asleep at night. Needless to say, I had sleep deprivation, often having to take sleep aids to settle my mind so that I could rest. The days were intense and full of unknowns and unplanned events. I remember thinking to myself, "I hope no one has to go through all this hell that I've had to go through."

So as my husband's trial began, I must say I was in somewhat of a robotic state, doing only what was necessary to stay afloat, and what I was instructed to do. To be honest, my focus was mainly on my children and making sure they would be okay. At this point in the marriage, we did have three wonderful children. Every single day I made every effort to give them a sense of normalcy in their lives even though our world was crumbling and closing in all around us.

The things that were shared on the first courtroom day were astounding. Probably, the most memorable statement came from his attorney's opening statement, *"Terry Hornbuckle broke the law of God, and not the law of the land."* While I was somewhat prepped for this defense, hearing it publicly really made me do some deep soul reflective *spiritual* thinking.

I thought we were pastors? I thought the law of God was just as important to us as the law of the land? Did not God's law carry as much weight, if not more, to us? The things I heard this day were shocking to me.

But this was just the beginning.

As the public was becoming aware of the horrid details of each of my husband's escapades, **so was I**. A lot of people assumed that I was knowledgeable of his actions, and the truth is that I had suspicion of strange behavior, but no proof, no confessions. So, these were very challenging and difficult days for me. Most days, it took all that I had to muster up strength to manage my children, and then get to the courthouse to make it through the trial. Each day, I would square my shoulders and hold my head high as I approached the courthouse knowing that I again would be greeted with cameras in my face and reporters lingering around. Somehow, even in the midst of these chaotic moments, I had to find a place of solace for my soul. And I did. All I could remember at the time was "Pray without ceasing." This would be a good time to pray and this scripture from 1 Thessalonians 5:17 sparked me to action.

I developed what many called in the prayer movement a "praying spirit" -- praying in my mind without uttering a word. Even while cameras were being shoved in my face and with reporters screaming at me, my spirit would automatically retreat into this prayer chamber. It seemed that every *single* second I had to do this; each second appearing to be longer than the last.

Many people often wondered how I made it through those years *and* the trial, and my answer is faith, trust and belief in God and 'consistent' prayer. Did I want to go off, get angry, scream and yell? Yes, but I had to be disciplined and self-controlled. I relied on God to help keep my composure.

Often, we, as leaders tell and teach our congregants how important it is to pray, but situations such as what I experienced do more than express the need to pray. PRAYER is vital to our life and our ability to get through tough times. I found out how truly important this was personally and I want you to understand that prayer must become a *major* tool that you learn to use in your life. God hears us when we pray and when we are in trouble that's a great time to pray!

Because of the types of pending allegations that my husband was accused of doing, many people did not know who to believe or what side to be on. What was the truth? What really happened? Should we believe the accusers? Should we believe Bishop Hornbuckle? Should we believe Mrs. Hornbuckle? Should we believe the attorneys? Or should we believe the media? This was so overwhelming for me.

I think the biggest disappointment for me was to actually have people attack me, my children and the church, when we, too, had been innocent bystanders. This was absolutely unbelievable. It was equally difficult for me to rationalize within my own mind how people, family and friends that I thought would be supportive of me and my innocent children, who also were affected by these rash behaviors, turned against us and cut us off. What did I do? Were not both me and our children casualties of this situation as well?

I had to learn how to embrace and overcome these challenges, as I knew every move I made was scrutinized, as well as, my demeanor was monitored closely! As if things were not bad enough, this simply added to my stress, knowing that I was under watchful eyes. The weight of the pressure was immense.

Yet, life still went on! My children had school and activities that required my attendance, and thank God, they made it through this ordeal. Life was not perfect by a long shot, but we all persevered. As well, the church still had to move forward.

My time was spent between the children and the church. To find some normalcy personally, most days when I was alone and had to be in the public, I would wear a baseball cap and sunglasses hiding from the shame and embarrassment. Hoping that no one would call my name and I would not have to talk to anyone; not having to explain the shambles of our life. It was during these times, that I found myself constantly searching for the SILENCE that would bring me PEACE.

Sitting in court for that period of time changed my life forever. After my husband was sentenced to prison, I immediately had to make decisions about the direction of life for me and my children. I had no time to grieve, life had to move forward.

That final day, I walked away from the courtroom, from the media, from the drama, IN SILENCE.

After settling from this ordeal, I soon begin to realize that I was on a path to really help people. I had always been passionate about helping people overcome life-altering situations, and now having lived it and at least somewhat having survived, I knew that now was the time -- the time for me to overcome the silence; the silence that I had hidden in for so many years.

So, I started on a new path of silence. And this is where I spent the next seven years...Healing...IN SILENCE.

IN SILENCE, being developed to help others *break their silence*.

201

Healing In Silence – The Path of Silence

Any type of crisis or loss, whether it involves personal possessions, a job or a family member, can be very stressful and overwhelming. When faced with a loss, crisis or life-changing event, you are suddenly thrust into an unfamiliar world, one that can be frightening and unsettling. And to make matters worse, many people stand at a distance to watch how you handle what you are going through. Why is it that more people watch than help? This can be quite puzzling, but I've come to the conclusion that many watch from a distance because they are not sure what to do or say. So instead they watch to see if you are able and capable of handling what you are going through.

As much as you may want others to take a closer look and help you through tough times, the reality is that YOU must be the one who makes a decision to take a closer look, confront where you are and choose to do something about your situation. You must learn how to respond and react for yourself. Also you must realize that your reaction directly affects others who are watching, so you always want to present the correct response. So, knowing how to make it through the first few days or hours can provide great comfort in the midst of a crisis.

You must accept that crises are a normal part of life - some are mild and soon forgotten; others are intense and life-changing. Because they are disruptive, all crises require you to respond and to make decisions. Almost always, there is emotional turmoil with accompanying physical reactions.

So, when you look at the definition of crisis it helps you to better understand what is required to make it through any ordeal that you face. A crisis is defined as: An unstable situation of extreme danger or difficulty; a point when a conflict reaches its highest tension and must be resolved. So, if you OWN your crisis you can change your path. You must start with your perception about your crisis, and then you must commit to working through the process so that you ultimately come through better, stronger and wiser; no longer making the same decisions, choices or reactions.

When you have a crisis or suffer loss, you might recognize that there are three phases *in* the experience:

> ➤ **First comes shock**. You feel stunned, have difficulty believing that the event has

really happened, maybe confused about what to do next, and sometimes overwhelmed by emotion. This is when you feel like you've had the wind knocked out of you and you can't catch your breath.

➢ Next, there is a phase of **initial coping**. Depending on the severity of the crisis, this phase may continue for a few weeks, for several months, or longer. The person in crisis struggles to accept and cope with the reality of what has happened. Often there is anxiety, insecurity, insensitivity to others, inefficiency (including a decline of work performance), and all of the emotions that come with grieving and being sorrowful about the course of events. Decision making is important at this time, but difficult. The person in crisis may wonder if he or she will be able to cope, to get beyond the crisis, and ever be happy and fulfilled again.

> Eventually, most people move slowly and cautiously into a **third phase, adjustment**. This is where the reality of the crisis event is eventually accepted emotionally and intellectually, anxiety tends to lessen, new behaviors and ways of living become routine, and the person is able to move forward with life.

So, once you get through these initial phases, then what must you do? If you are a Christian, you have the Word of God to stand on. As believers, we put our hope in Christ. It's a comfort to know that Christ gives hope and comfort in times of stressful circumstances. This is not a new strategy.

For centuries, people have found help and consolation in the pages of Scripture. It tells us in *2 Corinthians 12:9, "My grace (My favor and loving-kindness and mercy) is enough for you [sufficient against any danger and enables you to bear the trouble manfully]; for My strength and power are made perfect (fulfilled and completed) and show themselves most effective in [your] weakness"* (AMP).

And so we benefit from the peace that comes from Christ and from the strength that He gives. *Isaiah 43:2-3 states, "When you pass through the waters, I will be with you; and when you pass through the rivers, they will not sweep over you. When you walk through the fire, you will not be burned; the flames will not set you ablaze. For I am the LORD, your God, the Holy One of Israel."* *(AMP)* **I take great comfort in knowing that God is always with me; even during the most trying**

times! All we have to do is just rest in HIM; and trust that He will bring us through whatever situations we are faced with.

We also benefit from the warmth and acceptance of fellow believers who show love, and who avoid trying to create answers to difficult "Why?" questions. It's best and most helpful in the midst of crises, when other people are simply present, available, and praying for you.

When you are able to talk about your feelings, including your confusion and anger, there is less likelihood that trouble-producing bitterness will develop. The pain and memories may never go away, but we can grow through crises and, with the help and guidance of the Holy Spirit, we move on with our lives.

As our world continues to experience devastation and destruction, we must all learn how to cope and get through tough times. Therefore, next time instead of watching from a distance, whether it's you or someone else who's faced with a life challenge or any kind of a loss, it is helpful to remember some of the basic, practical common sense steps that can be taken.

This **COPING STRATEGY LIST** is what I personally applied during my crisis and like to recommend to people to keep them moving during the initial phase of any kind of crisis:

- **Process Your Feelings!** Take it one hour at a time, one day at a time, if need be, one moment at a time.

- **Take Care Of Yourself!** Get enough sleep or at least enough rest. If you are exhausted you won't be able to process information effectively.

- **Try and maintain some type of a normal routine as best as possible.** This is of utmost importance if you have children. Their daily routines should continue as best as possible.

- **Remember that regular exercise helps relieve stress and tension**. Even if it's just a walk or relaxation exercises.

- **Eat a balanced diet.** Limit high calorie and junk food. Drink plenty of water.

- **Avoid using alcohol, medications or other drugs in excess or to mask the pain.** Once the effects of alcohol and drugs wears off, you still have to face the facts!

- **Find Support!** Talk to others, especially those who have lived through and survived similar experiences. Be with people who comfort, sustain and recharge you.

- **Be Patient with Yourself!** Give yourself time and permission to heal. You will have some challenging days, and that's perfectly alright. Just don't let those challenges begin to weigh you down.

- **Find creative ways- journal, paint, photograph, build, draw, and spend quality time with family, read, walk or workout- to express intense feelings.** I personally found comfort in working or organizing during challenging times.

- **Remember the coping skills you have used to survive former losses.** Draw upon these inner strengths again.

- **Seek help if you need to!** Don't be ashamed to see a licensed professional, or speak with your pastor, counselor, or a person of wisdom.

- **Focus! Focus! Focus**! Focus only on what's important!

- **PRAY!** And wait to hear from God on what to do!

To better manage life, it certainly would be great to know when trouble plans to come. But we don't. And it doesn't ever come at a convenient time. It actually tends to come at times of inconvenience - as an interruption when we least expect it! The truth is that as much as we desire for things to be just "right" in life - the reality is that there will be troubles. I like to ask this question, "Life is going to happen and when it does, will you be ready?" In the midst of your life and dreams coming to pass and things being wonderful learn to be aware! Don't be fearful, but be aware. Trouble may be lurking around the corner at any time. It's just a fact, that's how the enemy works. He's really a coward. He tends to trip you up to take you out and keep you from reaching your great destiny. And he always comes after you when you least expect it. Beware! Be Vigilant.

From my own experience, I want you to know that the way I made it through was by relying on God. My source of strength and courage came totally from God. It is through taking God's principles and applying them that you can, with the help of God, turn things around.

I also believe that everything you need to overcome your situation is already inside of you waiting to be activated. Just make a choice to apply God's Word to your situation. Just do it. That's a big time quote we all hear used in Nike's ads and they are right. But with the greater source – God – nothing is impossible.

Jesus said in the Word found in *Mark 10:27,* *"With men it is impossible, but not with God; for all things are possible with God.'*

It's a fact that most people often don't rise above life's challenges, because they simply don't know how to handle the situations they are faced with. Taking the right steps in the right direction when faced with difficulty can be a challenge in itself. However, if you can learn to follow a process (God's process, the counseling process, etc.), even in the midst of bad times, you can get back to the good times.

What you cannot do, is sit back and pretend it doesn't exist. That's called denial. And you can't stay in denial because it will get you nowhere. You have to confront where you are!

To those of us that profess to be Christians, God's Word is clear on what we must do! We must Trust HIM to see us through! So if and when your life seems bent out of shape and crooked, like mine was, may you find this scripture comforting, *"Trust in the LORD with all your heart and lean not on your own understanding; ⁶ in all your ways submit to him, and he will make your paths straight." Proverbs 3: 5-6*

BREAKING FREE – BREAK THE SILENCE TIP

If you've faced or are currently facing a crisis of any kind, it is my hope that you will learn, first of all, that even in the midst of what appears to be hopelessness, you can ALWAYS find HOPE! It is my prayer that you learn THE PROCESS of how to walk the path toward totally rebuilding your life, even with others watching. The beauty of it all is that through your life – others will hopefully learn that they too can make it through the challenges of life with God!

Take the following steps:

- Believe that your situation can and will change

- Trust God! With God you can make it thru the initial phase

- Confront your situation

- Review your Coping List daily

- Take practical steps of finding the right kind of support to make positive change in your life:

  1. spiritually (from the Word and spiritual counsel),

  2. emotionally (from family and authentic friends),

  3. and financially (through family and friends, and/or agencies that can help you through your transition).

*The secret of success is
learning how to use pain and
pleasure instead of having pain
and pleasure use you. If you do
that, you're in control of your
life. If you don't, life controls
you.*

Tony Robbins

VICTORY
is always possible for the
person who refuses to stop
fighting.

Napoleon Hill

Chapter 10

THE POWER OF
SILENT VICTORY

A New Life!

P eople say it's been seven years of silence. I see it as seven years of hard work and rebuilding of my life. While I have been silent, I have been working. I have spent the time working very hard to rebuild my life, my children's lives, my congregation's life, and the lives of those that have watched from afar. Many throughout the country may have thought that I disappeared, but those around the community I live in have watched as I have diligently worked to rebuild what had been assumedly destroyed.

What am I saying? This time SILENCE was used in a constructive way. My silence was used in a very useful way. It gave me an opportunity to allow my soul (the soul can be described as your personality, your thoughts, your attitudes and what makes you unique) to be in a state of healing and rest. The silence now gave me opportunity to quiet my inner person and walk through the healing process. For me, it was a reflective time to find a productive way to help my children heal, to keep them on course. It gave me an opportunity to clear my thoughts, to focus on finding a new creative voice, and for me to learn to be content and at peace. This time silence was used to rebuild a hurting church. In this silence, I got a new, redefined plan from God on how to use this horrible situation for good. It wasn't always easy, but with vigor and determination, I moved forward.

My strategy is simple: I live by Matthew 6:33, "Seek the Kingdom of God above all else, and live righteously, and he will give you everything you need."

Then, I applied key life principles. For example:

1) I have learned how to establish clear direction while going through tough times by waiting to hear from God on what to do next.

2) Once I hear from God, I make a secure commitment to move into the position and alignment of what HE has said. It can be hard sometimes. But it's through prayer and meditation that I can get clear. As I spend time with God, that's where I get the strength, the energy that I need personally so that I can motivate and inspire others to overcome the obstacles that will surely arise.

3) I also live my life knowing that I'm here to make a difference. So serving others is really important. I choose to look for opportunities to give back or as they say now – pay it forward.

So, I am paying it forward. I'm doing what God has called me to do. My children are and will continue to come into their own. Their responsibilities right now are getting their education. My daughter, Rachel, started a foundation where she collects prom dresses and gives them to other young ladies with a need. We don't care what the need is. You don't have to be low-income. A lot of people are going through difficult times and simply need help. So, why not help others if you are able. With Rachel, in the midst of our troubles, God showed her a new idea, a new purpose. She knows now because of our experience, what it's like to go through a crisis, to have your life shattered and not be able to afford the dress you really want.

People don't think about how challenging it was for my children. They, too, had to make adjustments and sacrifices, and out of our crisis, we have all chosen to live forward!

Thank God all three of my children made it through this ordeal! We had our share of ups and downs, but with focus and determination, they too, learned how to maneuver through the process of negative circumstances. I taught them to rely on God, and to trust that HE would guide them to their destiny. All three are in college; two of them received full scholarships. The beauty and blessing of this is that they all were able to continue in life and achieve their goals in the midst of turmoil.

If you get stuck in the past or you allow your crisis to define you, you miss out on the opportunity to grow and develop. It keeps you bound and going nowhere, robbing you of the chance to live a good life. Every day that I awake, I thank God for the new day, the new opportunity to live an abundant life!

No longer married, I had to move forward in life. I was legally divorced on February 14, 2011. Yes, Valentine's Day – I just figure God has a sense of humor and wanted me to vividly remember my date of change. I filed in October of 2009 and spent almost two years in mediation and court, while still moving forward with life, raising my children, and doing what God called me to do – empowering lives. And I think it's important to note here, that I should have and could have been quite bitter. I had no support, and as a single mom with no child support or alimony it was quite hard at times. In fact, faced with financial ruin due to the scandal and a lengthy divorce it would have made more sense to give up. But I chose not to do so.

It was difficult, and most people wanted to know why I waited so long to file for divorce, especially with biblical grounds. Well, what's interesting about my choice is this. When our world fell apart, I remember saying to the Lord, "I don't understand what's going on right now. Please give me wisdom and peace!" Lots of people said, "You need to divorce him, you have grounds for divorce." Call me odd, but I'm a true nurturer, so the wellbeing of others affected by all that had happened was more important to me. I chose to simply remain silent and get to work. I chose to put my personal life on the back burner for a season. Rather than focus on what I was going through personally, I knew I had to care for my children and care for the people God had entrusted into our care. I knew that the time for attention to personal matters would come later.

It took approximately the first four years for me to rebuild, to provide this care, to get things somewhat stabilized. I was the set leader, the head of the household. No support from a denomination, no other career (I left Corporate America in 1993), and no alimony or child support. It was up to me and I had to make certain that all was stabilized and everyone was okay. I at least wanted to attempt to bring stability as best as I could with the help of God.

During those rebuilding years, even with biblical grounds for divorce, in my heart, as a woman of faith, I also wanted to give the Lord room to bring restoration. I know this reasoning is hard to envision for some folk. If that was what HE (GOD) desired – I was willing! The only thing I asked of the Lord was to lead me, give me peace in my release when it was time and that I would have no regret. It was in those times of silence spent with God, that eventually; it became obvious that restoration of my marriage would not be possible. I walked away with peace and with no regret, knowing I had FULLY honored my marriage covenant. What I mean is that during the seven years of my forced separation, up until the divorce decree date and even now, I took the time to strengthen my personal relationship with God. I focused on my total and complete healing, my children, and my duties as a Pastor and Community Leader. I was not consumed with trying to find a replacement (another man) or some other vice outside of God to fill that void.

Actually, my perspective was that I had made a covenant before God concerning marriage, and until that agreement was dissolved by the courts (both heavenly and naturally), I was still married. I don't get it when people separate and start dating before they are divorced, but that's an entirely different subject.

Now, that I am 'single again' usually the next thing people want to know is will I marry again.

My reply, **"ABSOLUTELY!"** I loved marriage. I loved having a life partner. I loved the unity of FAMILY! I Love LIFE! And God has healed me so that I will be able to have another relationship at the right time. While I still have some things to walk through, I would welcome a partner who knows who he is in Christ, who loves me, and is confident and successful!

This is important to note, because after the experience of a bad relationship we must take the time to heal and not rush into another relationship.

LET HEALING BEGIN!

In order to get back to your own personal wholeness and well-being there are a few final steps you must take:

Step 1: Understand TRUE LOVE

The issues, feelings, responses and interactions involved in abusive relationships are very complex and difficult to understand. One important rule of measure for determining the health of a relationship, however, can be built on one simple truth – if it is TRUE LOVE, you should never be afraid. We have God's Word on it.

" There is no fear in love. But perfect love drives out fear, because fear has to do with punishment. The one who fears is not made perfect in love." **1 John 4:18**

God is love, and God's love for us is unconditional. God wants us to love Him, but gives us the freedom to make that choice. God does not force us to love Him. If someone is afraid in a relationship, then that is not love. Everyone

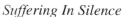

deserves a violence-free life. No one deserves to have to tolerate harsh words, put downs, name calling, belittling, or cussing. No one should be beaten and humiliated. If a person in a relationship has to worry that something he or she said or did might "set the person off," if he or she is always "walking on eggshells," or "waiting for the other shoe to drop," or afraid of how the person is going to verbally tear them down, then that is not love. Fear and love cannot coexist. If someone is afraid, it is because they are afraid of punishment and retribution. And that is not love, because there is no fear in love.

Christ has called us to be in peace, not fear: He has called us to follow His example of serving one another, not dominating each other. He has called us to Truth, not to deceit and hypocrisy. Christ has called us to **LOVE**, not to **ABUSE.** So, learn to receive **TRUE LOVE!** And trust that when you do, that's when you are able to **Break The SILENCE, Walk In FREEDOM, Be HEALED, and start the GREAT LIFE that is waiting for you!**

Step 2: FORGIVE!

You must forgive! In order to truly break free and to be totally healed, <u>you must forgive</u>. You have the power to forgive – and when you do, you will see that you have the strength to break the silence!

Forgive yourself and forgive others.

Early in the healing process, I was just mad one day. I was reading the scripture, the book of Galatians. I was mad at everyone. I was mad at my husband, the people around us, and my peers who turned their backs and no longer desired me to minister in their churches, seminars or conferences. I was mad at people who would not return my calls, judgmental folk and the media. I think I was even mad at God in some strange way. During this time, I really trusted no one. I had it out with God. He asked me, "Why are you so mad?" I said I have a right to be. You know what's going on in my life. You see how people are treating us. And you know what God said to me? No, you don't have a right. I said to God, "Excuse me? I have every right to be angry and mad and depressed."

He quickly reminded me of these words. "Forgive them." Of course I continued to rant and rave, "But God you don't understand. They hurt me. They betrayed me. They used me, I'm smarter than this. I don't think you understand how I feel....they....they...they." Again, HE reminded me, "Forgive them."

These two words changed my life, but in order to really walk out forgiveness, I ended up having to do a whole scripture search, study, meditation, and prayer in order to get to real forgiveness. It's not easy to forgive. The Lord made me get real quiet. He said, "Don't answer your critics, don't try to prove yourself, spend time with Me, attend your children's functions, go to church and stay home. Do this for six months."

What I learned? I had to heal and move on with life - so I chose to FORGIVE! It can be a hard thing to do—to completely let go of something painful and forgive the person who hurt you. Forgiveness is not always easy. And at times to forgive the one that inflicted our pain, can even feel more painful than the hurt we actually suffered.

But you must understand that forgiveness is a decision. You can hold on to what someone did to hurt you, you can keep your anger, resentment and thoughts of revenge or you can choose to embrace forgiveness and move forward.

Ask yourself this question, "If I don't let go and move forward, who and what is really controlling my life?" If you make a choice to stop defining your life by past hurts and pains, and choose to let go, it will take work; yet, you will eventually reach that place of forgiveness and be able to move forward with your life. You may have had no choice over what they did to you, but you definitely have a choice now how you're going to think and feel about it.

When you forgive, you in no way change the past—but you sure do change the future. Yet, there is no way to get to the future or to real peace in your life without forgiveness.

Forgiveness is simply making a commitment to a process of change. It's something that you can start right now, by making a choice to do so!

- Will you choose to forgive?
- Will you let go?

Once you decide to let go; you can move forward in your life!

In the words of - **Maya Angelou "We may encounter many defeats but we must not be defeated."**

And YOU are not defeated!

Lewis B. Smedes said these words, "You will know that forgiveness has begun when you recall those who hurt you and feel the power to wish them well."

It will take time, but Just keep working the process and you will reach that place of wholeness just like I did.

I reached my place of healing and now It is my passion to help people understand that they don't have to live defeated lives! I want people to learn that life will challenge them from time to time, but with the right tools they can challenge it back! That's what I did to take back my life and it worked!!! No one, and I do mean no one, should have to **suffer in silence**.

As we started this journey, if you recall, my prayer was that by you reading this book that you would find the strength to break your silence **and** suffering or help someone else to do so. I hope you have found the courage to speak out and change your situation. I hope that you have found strength to be able to regain the life you once loved and live again.

Therefore, it is my prayer that you have learned THE PROCESS of how to walk the path toward totally rebuilding your life by BREAKING THE SILENCE AND LETTING HEALING BEGIN!

I broke the
SILENCE,
I'm no longer
bound by the
suffering!
I've HEALED and
I'm moving forward

CONCLUSION

I think the best way to close this book out is with a newspaper article that one of the local private newspapers wrote about our church.

Agape Christian Fellowship: NOT The House That Hornbuckle Built by Melissa Norris (Reprinted with Permission by Manna Express).

> ***DALLAS*** *– A year and a half after the story broke on March 11, 2005 of the horrible offenses of the Bishop Terry Hornbuckle, former pastor of the Agape Christian Fellowship Church, Arlington, TX, the healing finally begins with the verdict and sentencing over. With speculation and opinions flying about what the remaining church members and now sole pastor, Pastor/Mrs. Renee Hornbuckle should do, who can say without actually being in each members' shoes, God forbid. Recently, I reluctantly obeyed a sudden unction to visit the Agape Christian Fellowship Church. To my surprise, no*

sooner had I driven onto the parking lot did I recognize that these were the die-hard members, the ones who would say that this is my church no matter who is the pastor. I entered the sanctuary as the praise and worship leader led the congregation in a chorus of, "It's All About You Jesus," when God began to speak saying, "I Am Here, this is NOT the house that Hornbuckle built; this is My House and I Am Here. They are here to worship Me and not a man. If I had killed Hornbuckle (instead of allowing him to be exposed) the same would have left. Those who left, left because of a man, those who stayed, stayed to worship Me; and because they stayed, I will increase this house and set it on a hill to be a light unto the nation. This will become a house of deliverance for those bound by sexual sins even as they enter the doors." The presence of God was so strong in that place that I could hardly stand. Being there, I could sense why the members stayed, the pastors could be replaced like humans often are, but "this" is their Father's House, and He is still "here". We should not be surprised that a man of God, a man first, could fail so miserably. Many do as badly and worse without ever *becoming media spectacles. The Bible tells us that many of our spiritual leaders will pray us into heaven and healing, yet Jesus will deny ever knowing them in the final analysis of their own lives, and as I like to say – "burst Hell wide open".*

Pastor Renee mounted the podium with excitement like you could not imagine and even leaped with joy, or leaped for joy. If she keeps that up, she will be fine in no time. While the congregation was encouraged to forgive and restore one overtaken in a fault by Pastors Tommy and Brenda Todd, who arrived unannounced and shared a message, Pastor Renee gave a confirming nod. When Pastor Renee was given the podium to preach, she confirmed by her notes that they had, by the Spirit of God, already ministered what God had given her to preach. While we cannot expect her to live in the spirit realm 24 hours a day, 7 days a week without feeling the pain of what she has personally endured, at least she knows "from whence cometh" her help. Whether she remains the pastor after the 4-month trial period, or takes a rest from the public eye for herself and

243

her children, she has endured like a good soldier and will never be forsaken. As a prominent leader of women, I am sure that in due season, she will share how she was able to stand as she did throughout the ordeal. I feel so proud of the members of Agape that I am humbled in their presence for they are true worshippers of the Lord Jesus and not a man.

There is
VICTORY
in the
SILENCE
that
HEALS!

APPENDIXES

SAFETY PLANNING

Safety planning for someone involved in an abusive relationship is a necessary and important step. Planning can be used while you are still with your abuser or after the relationship has ended. While still in an abusive relationship, your safety is of primary importance.

Safety Plan Guidelines

These safety suggestions have been compiled from safety plans distributed by state domestic violence coalitions from around the country. Following these suggestions is not a guarantee of safety, but could help to improve your safety situation.

245

Personal Safety with an Abuser

- Identify your partner's use and level of force so that you can assess danger to you and your children before it occurs.

- Try to avoid an abusive situation by leaving.

- Identify safe areas of the house where there are no weapons and there are ways to escape. If arguments occur, try to move to those areas.

- Don't run to where the children are, as your partner may hurt them as well.

- If violence is unavoidable, make yourself a small target; dive into a corner and curl up into a ball with your face protected and arms around each side of your head, fingers entwined.

- If possible, have a phone accessible at all times and know what numbers to call for help. Know where the nearest pay phone is located. Know the phone number to your local battered women's shelter. Don't be afraid to call the police.

- Let trusted friends and neighbors know of your situation and develop a plan and visual signal for when you need help.

- Teach your children how to get help. Instruct them not to get involved in the violence between you and your partner. Plan a code word to signal to them that they should get help or leave the house.

- Tell your children that violence is never right, even when someone they love is being violent. Tell them that neither you, nor they, are at fault or are the cause of the violence, and that when anyone is being violent, it is important to stay safe.

- Practice how to get out safely. Practice with your children.

- Plan for what you will do if your children tell your partner of your plan or if your partner otherwise finds out about your plan.

- Keep weapons like guns and knives locked away and as inaccessible as possible.

- Make a habit of backing the car into the driveway and keeping it fueled. Keep the driver's door unlocked and others locked — for a quick escape.

- Try not to wear scarves or long jewelry that could be used to strangle you.

- Create several plausible reasons for leaving the house at different times of the day or night.

- Call a domestic violence hotline periodically to assess your options and get a supportive understanding ear.

Getting Ready to Leave

- Keep any evidence of physical abuse, such as pictures.

- Know where you can go to get help; tell someone what is happening to you.

- If you are injured, go to a doctor or an emergency room and report what happened to you. Ask that they document your visit.

- Plan with your children and identify a safe place for them, like a room with a lock or a friend's house where they can go for help. Reassure them that their job is to stay safe, not to protect you.

- Contact your local battered women's shelter and find out about laws and other resources available to you before you have to use them during a crisis.

- Keep a journal of all violent incidences, noting dates, events and threats made, if possible.

- Acquire job skills or take courses at a community college as you can.

- Try to set money aside or ask friends or family members to hold money for you.

General Guidelines for Leaving an Abusive Relationship

- You may request a police stand-by or escort while you leave.

- If you need to sneak away, be prepared.

- Make a plan for how and where you will escape.

- Plan for a quick escape.

- Put aside emergency money as you can.

- Hide an extra set of car keys.

- Pack an extra set of clothes for yourself and your children and store them at a trusted friend or neighbor's house. Try to avoid using the homes of next-door neighbors, close family members and mutual friends.

- Take with you important phone numbers of friends, relatives, doctors, schools, etc., as well as other important items, including:
  - Driver's license
  - Regularly needed medication
  - Credit cards or a list of credit cards you hold yourself or jointly
  - Pay stubs
  - Checkbooks and information about bank accounts and other assets

- If time is available, also take:
    - Citizenship documents (such as your passport, green card, etc.)
    - Titles, deeds and other property information
    - Medical records
    - Children's school and immunization records
    - Insurance information
    - Copy of marriage license, birth certificates, will and other legal documents
    - Verification of social security numbers
    - Welfare identification valued pictures, jewelry or personal possessions
    - You may also create a false trail. Call motels, real estate agencies and schools in a town at least six

hours away from where you plan to relocate. Ask questions that require a call back to your house in order to leave phone numbers on record.

After Leaving the Abusive Relationship

If getting a restraining order and the offender is leaving:

- Change your locks and phone number.
- Change your work hours and route taken to work.
- Change the route taken to transport children to school.
- Keep a certified copy of your restraining order with you at all times.
- Inform friends, neighbors and employers that you have a restraining order in effect.

- Give copies of the restraining order to employers, neighbors and schools along with a picture of the offender.
- Call law enforcement to enforce the order.

If you leave:

- Consider renting a post office box or using the address of a friend for your mail.
- Be aware that addresses are on restraining orders and police reports.
- Be careful to whom you give your new address and phone number.
- Change your work hours, if possible.
- Alert school authorities of the situation.
- Consider changing your children's schools.
- Reschedule appointments that the offender is aware of.
- Use different stores and frequent different social spots.

- Alert neighbors and request that they call the police if they feel you may be in danger.
- Talk to trusted people about the violence.
- Replace wooden doors with steel or metal doors. Install security systems if possible.
- Install a motion sensitive lighting system.
- Tell people you work with about the situation and have your calls screened by one receptionist if possible.
- Tell people who take care of your children who can pick up your children. Explain your situation to them and provide them with a copy of the restraining order.
- Call the telephone company to request caller ID. Ask that your phone number be blocked so that if you call anyone, neither your partner nor anyone else will be able to get your new, unlisted phone number.

Additional Types of Abuse To Be Familiar With

- **Types of Verbal & Mental Abuse**

  Jun 22, 2010 | By Harold E. Sconiers

  Abuse is an excessive or wrongful harm, voluntarily caused to one person by another. Abuse can come from any person and show itself in a variety of forms. Victims of verbal and mental abuse often fail to perceive the true aggression to which they have been beset, and the damage is most often to mental and emotional well-being, imperceptible to the naked eye. Learning to recognize the types of verbal and mental abuse can help you or someone you know.

- **Economic Abuse**

  Economic or financial abuse is the attempt, made by any person, to deny another the right to resources, earnings or the pursuit of self-sufficiency. An abuser will often use such tactics to force the victim into a position of dependency. By withholding resources, the abuser creates an environment in which the victim must rely solely on the abuser for life's necessities. Financially abusive maneuvers include those that directly interfere with a person's occupational performance, withholding information regarding the state of shared financial affairs and demanding that even moderate spending be justified to and subject to the abuser's authority.

• **Intimidation**

Intimidation is the act of using threats to instill fear in another. These threats may be either spoken or implied, through words, gestures, looks or behaviors. Intimidation can also be applied through the tone of voice, subtle sarcasms and retorts of an abuser intent on backing the victim into a mental corner.

Allowing yourself to be intimidated, over time, has a corrosive effect on your self-esteem. You may lose confidence in your ability to make personal choices and seek to determine how your abuser would respond before making decisions. Acting in this manner then diminishes your self-esteem even further.

- **Criticism**

When you are unjustly criticized by another person, it can feel as if your sense of self is under attack. Unlike constructive feedback, which is presented in a spirit of aid and good-will, criticism is constructed in a way that de-values its recipient's worth. It contains an implication that the victim is inherently incapable, incompetent or flawed in some way. Criticism is often masked as an attempt at humor or an effort to look out for the victim's "best interest". However, it's true meaning is felt whether or not it is revealed.

IMPORTANT

Remember if you or someone you know needs help, please call:

National Domestic Violence Hotline

at 1-800-799-SAFE (7233),

1-800-787-3224 (TTY),

or your local Domestic Violence

Center **to talk with someone.**

Don't wait – call NOW!

REFERENCES

Freda D. Doxey LPC
Licensed Professional Counselor
The Doxey Group, Inc.

National Coalition Against Domestic Abuse:
Economic Abuse

Laurence C. Smith, Jr., PhD: Criticism- Our Disease

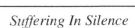

Made in the USA
Columbia, SC
27 February 2019